the Mama Manual

To the amazing
Annabel Karmel,
What an honour
to meet you!
Best,
Nakita x

the Mama Manual

How busy mums get organised

Nakita Attard Vassallo

the Mama Manual - How busy mums get organised

Printed in Malta

ISBN 978-99957-1-311-9

Typeset and cover design by Keith Chetcuti, FatBat
www.fatbat.design

Cover and inside pages Illustrations by Ruth Zammit DeBono © Chic Odyssey illustrations, www.chicodyssey.com

Editing and proofreading by Elizabeth Cortis, Proofreading Malta, www.proofreadingmalta.com

To my husband Neil and my two wonderful children.

Neil, thank you for believing in me, for your encouragement to follow my dreams, and your constant love and support. Yanik, you taught me so many things about being a mama, and you Nina, made our life busier and happier. Without you all, the Mama Manual would not have been born.

Contents

ACKNOWLEDGEMENTS

I would like to express my gratitude to the following people who made this book possible.

To my editor, Elizabeth Cortis (Proofreading Malta), who took on this project as if it were her own. Thank you for being so enthusiastic from the very beginning, and for your expertise through to the very end. It was a delight to work with you!

To the very talented Keith Chetcuti (FatBat), who contributed in so many ways! First and foremost, he has created the Mama Manual logo which represents every aspect of the brand in a graceful and feminine way. He also designed and typeset this book and made it look totally gorgeous! Keith, I am forever indebted to you for the invaluable advice you have given me in relation to digital marketing, and any technical stumbling blocks I have encountered along the way. Thank you for your words of wisdom, encouragement, and friendship.

To my amazing illustrator, Ruth Zammit DeBono (Chic Odyssey). We met by chance and it was meant to be! Thank you for giving life to the cover by artfully placing me on it, in front of our majestic Triton Fountain found in Valletta, Malta. Each illustration you see before every chapter has been lovingly illustrated by Ruth.

To the incredible community of ladies I connect with every day on the Mama Manual social media pages. When the book's first draft was completed, I realised I had so much more to say, and what better way to say it than on social media? I poured my heart out to you because I wanted all of you to know that despite the daily struggles, YOU matter. Thank you for being so receptive, engaged, and for being a part of the Mama Manual community.

To my family and friends. Thank you for showing up and applauding me. Thank you for your continued support, constant encouragement, and your love.

To my husband, Neil, for patiently listening to me go on and on about this book. Thank you for believing in me and for urging me to take on this project before it had even begun. I am grateful to have you by my side. This book would have definitely never been published without you.

Last but not least, to my children, Yanik and Nina. Thank you for inspiring me to be the best version of myself so that I can be an amazing mama to you.

INTRODUCTION

Back in the day, before I became a mum and a wife, I used to be so disorganised. I can imagine my mother chuckling as she reads this!

I was so disorganised I did not even dare to admit it to anyone outside of my household. I had the time to be so, and, admittedly, I was lazy. I had plenty and way too much time for myself despite spending half of my days looking for something I had misplaced.

Having a family and a home to care for changed my life. Disorganisation was a luxury I could no longer afford. It was high time I pulled my socks up. My day still consisted of the same number of hours, but my to-do list had multiplied tenfold. I was determined to not just tick things off my list of chores and duties, but to have time for myself and to live a full, happy life.

Taking baby steps, I started to improve by gradually getting organised. I prioritised what was most important to me and brainstormed all the ways I could possibly improve in those specific areas before moving on to the next part of my life, and then the next.

As I settled into a routine I evolved into the opposite of what I had once been—a savvy, organised being. I taught myself a myriad of time-saving tips, organisation strategies, and shortcuts to save myself precious time, whilst not skimping on quality. I learnt to actually get more done in a better way, and in less time!

Where I am today is a happy place thanks to healthy habits and hacks that allow me to lead a reasonably organised life. I prioritise what's most important to me. I have a successful career and spend plenty of time with my family, have time for myself, enjoy blogging on a daily basis and I have even found the time to write this book!

There is no magic involved; it's all about having the right daily routine, a routine that I will share with you and which you can easily adapt to, slowly but surely.

The good news is that if you lead a hectic life and run frantically between work and home only to cook dinner at 9 p.m. you are still in time to change your habits and adapt to your new lifestyle thanks to better time management.

The aim is to live, and not to exist. Your kids are only young once and you need to enjoy them. Don't let the days fly by only to look back and realise that your days have only been made up of mayhem and chores. Spend time with yourself and don't forget who you are.

USING THIS MANUAL

If you are lucky enough to be blessed with a girlfriend or partner who has bought you this book while you're expecting, you can take all the time in the world to pore over the book page by page, preferably with a cup of tea in hand, and your feet propped up on a footstool.

You might have been fortunate enough to stumble upon my blog or social media pages, or you might have even looked for inspiration to get yourself sorted before motherhood took centre stage.

If you are already a mum and lead an impossibly hectic life, don't lose heart! Remember that this book was written by a fellow working mum who was once in your shoes! I can promise you that the strategies you will read about will help you lead a less stressful life whilst enjoying your family, your home, and yourself more than ever. It is well worth investing some down time each evening to read this book.

Remember that practice makes perfect! If you 'fail' to pick up a habit or find yourself in an unplanned head over heels week and feel like you've lost it all and are back where you started—stop! Take a deep breath, recompose yourself, and start again. Nothing's perfect, and no one is. Stumbling blocks are just that: stumbling blocks.

This book has been written especially for those who are really busy. Even just a few minutes a day are guaranteed to add value to your busy lifestyle. Key points at the end of each chapter will help you refresh your memory and kick-start your new and improved daily routine.

Try to implement the suggested strategies as you go along. Don't give up; everything will start to fall into place once your time is better managed across the board.

Good luck, you're on your way to a happier, more fulfilling life!

CHAPTER 1
SETTING YOURSELF UP FOR SUCCESS

"You will never be completely ready. Start from wherever you are."
—C.J. Hayden, MCC

WHERE TO START: BUY TIME

They say money doesn't buy happiness, but it certainly buys you time. More time on your hands will give you more freedom to do more of what you want.

There are several products and services which you can purchase or make use of. They will save you so much time that you will wonder how you used to manage to do it all without them!

If you can afford it, try not to skimp on savings here. The breathing space you will gain will allow you to live a slower-paced, more intentionally planned lifestyle.

TOP GAME-CHANGERS

The products

1. Large freezer

A week after we bought our chest freezer I was already raving about how in the world we used to live without it. The tiny freezer which formed part of our fridge could hardly hold a week's essentials.

Why not cook once and serve twice? Having ample space in the freezer also means that you are able to stock up on items which you use regularly, having to make fewer trips to the shops.

There are two types of freezers available: upright and chest. Chest freezers offer more storage but it can get a bit tedious when it comes to looking for something inside them. Upright freezers have drawers which are handy but take up a lot of space. You also need to consider the space you will be placing the freezer in. Is it more ideal to have a top opening door or a front one?

Freezers typically come in four sizes: compact, small, medium, and large. Unless you have a large kitchen or garage the size you opt for will depend on the space you have. Keep in mind that the closer the freezer is to the kitchen, the better. It is better to opt for a medium-sized freezer two metres away from the kitchen rather than a large freezer in the garage.

2. Tumble dryer

Clothes take so much longer to dry in humid weather. If you have no outdoor area, you might have even had to hang up clothes in the bedroom or living room and switch on a fan, which is very unsightly and impractical. If you do have an outdoor area, you've probably experienced hanging a wash out to dry only to have it rain a few hours later!

A tumble dryer can seem expensive but can be such a huge help. Say goodbye to the days when you have to check the weather before doing the laundry! You are now able to throw them from the washing machine into the tumble dryer, and you're done!

If you did not plan for a tumble dryer, do not despair! No special plumbing or prepping is involved. There are two types available: vented tumble dryers or condenser tumble dryers.

Vented tumble dryers come with a hose which you can permanently pass through a wall to the outside (you can also temporarily hang it out of a window or doorway, if physically possible). Condenser tumble dryers do not need a vent, because the water is collected in a little tank which can be easily removed and emptied when the indicator light switches on.

Another option is a washer/dryer, which essentially is one machine which launders your clothes from the washing stage right through to the drying stage in one appliance. The only downside to this is that if you have a fault in either your dryer or your washing machine, you are unable to use the other one since they are one and the same.

3. Dishwasher

"It doesn't take that long to wash plates of a family of four."

True. Imagine this, however: You arrive home with a hungry toddler in tow. You heat up a bowl of soup, left over from the previous night's dinner. You make yourself a cuppa which you drink while you feed her. Your older son comes into the kitchen to make a snack before he rushes off to an extracurricular activity. He finishes his snack and puts the plate, cutlery, and glass into the sink and runs off. Your daughter finishes her soup. The bowl goes into the sink, the cutlery too. The leftover soup is now finished so the pot goes into the sink as well, followed by the mug and teaspoon in quick succession.

Result? A sink full of dirty plates.

Now imagine the same scenario with a dishwasher. Everything goes straight into the dishwasher, door closed, kitchen spick-and-span. What I also love about this appliance is that the area next to the sink is always clear, and should you have a load ready to be unloaded you can forget about it and unload it when the time is right. Always open the dishwasher as soon as it is ready, to avoid condensation. Be patient and wait for the dishes to completely air dry before unloading—that will save you another step: the drying part!

If you're entertaining, it is so much easier to plop everything right in! I've always hated cleaning after having friends over; it really spoils all the fun!

4. Microwave

We lived for years without one of these, but it's an absolute essential if you have kids. You can use your microwave for so many things!

If you are bottle feeding, you can buy an inexpensive micro-wave steriliser which will not take up any counter space and is as easy as ABC to use. Once your kid switches to cow's milk, a quick 30 seconds in the microwave will result in room temperature milk. I do this with the milk in a microwave-safe bottle, no teat on.

More microwave uses

*   Older kids can very easily heat up plates of food if left to their own devices. Babysitters or family members

watching your smaller children can have the little one's food prepared in the fridge, and it would be ready to feed after a quick reheat.

- Heating up microwavable plush animals for your sweet-hearts (they're so cosy; my daughter adores hers!).

- Potatoes cook much quicker in the microwave. The average-sized potato cooks in about four minutes. Remember to prick the potatoes and turn them over halfway through.

- If you're in a hurry and need to cook something in the oven that cooks from frozen (like oven chips or pie), defrost it in the microwave while the oven heats up, then transfer to the oven. This saves so much time!

- Sticky, stinky kitchen sponge? No problem! Leave to soak in white vinegar and place in the microwave for one minute. This disinfects and will also remove any smells.

- Last but not least, my favourite - to reheat your tea or coffee for the umpteenth time! Definite mama hack!

5. Slow cooker

I bought my first slow cooker after reading about this marvellous piece of equipment on the internet. It is ideal for working mums, or anyone else for that matter. I must admit, this is my favourite piece of kitchen equipment/gadget, and if I had to give up everything in my house bar one item it would undoubtedly be this!

I now have quite a list of delicious recipes which take little time to prepare and cook throughout the day for us to find a warm dinner ready for the evening.

Choose one of the larger versions so you will be able to freeze extra portions, and opt for a longer rectangular or oval shape which can also hold roasts and bakes more successfully. Some of my favourite recipes can be found in Chapter 3. The slow cooker is designed to simmer food over a number of hours, so there is no risk of your food getting burnt. It is especially great for stews and curries; I also make the most delicious soups, risottos and roasts very successfully!

Since I have bought my first slow cooker I have also recently upgraded to a newer version, which is a multi-cooker. It also steams, bakes, roasts and can be used for sautéing. It is a brilliant little machine which I now use at least five times a week. The sautéing function means that I can now also prep ingredients inside it and put it away in the fridge when I am not just slow cooking, but prepping for other recipes too. Several family members and friends have taken my advice and gone ahead and got a slow cooker for themselves after hearing me rave about it. It's also dishwasher safe—another plus!

6. Vacuum cleaner

Need I go into the specifics of how messy kids are and how easy it is to clean up after them with a vacuum cleaner?

The wired kind are more powerful than the wireless version. Choose one with an extra-long cord if you opt for the wired version.

There are also the bagless and the bag type. Both carry advantages and disadvantages. It is obviously much quicker to empty and clean the bag type since all you need to do is remove and throw away the bag. The bagless type does take some minutes to empty and clean; however, there is no risk of running out of bags and no extra costs involved in buying them either.

7. Smartphone

One might be quite perplexed at the mention of investing in a smartphone to make life simpler. Right after my slow cooker, my next favourite gadget is my smartphone. If truth be told, my smartphone is a very strong contender! The smartphone is as handy as a traditional diary or notebook but offers so much more. The biggest bonus that smartphones offer is that appointments, reminders and applications can be shared across devices and with other users.

Real-time updating with my husband for a multitude of things and the resulting coordination between us is literally a lifesaver. The fact that I can access my calendar, recipes, appointments, and more from the office, the kitchen, the car—anywhere—is a huge bonus! I enter reminders into my calendar for every little thing! Why try to remember everything when you can assign it to a day and time in your digital calendar?

ORGANISATION TIP

The first 'all-day' entry for every single day is what we are eating for dinner. Other typical entries which save me time include 'take chicken out of the freezer', or 'print school papers' or 'place chequebook in handbag'.

8. Voice-activated hands-free kit

Depending on the make of your smartphone, your phone comes with a personal assistant (PA). If you haven't used it already, check out the phone's manual to discover what you need to say to prompt your own PA to answer. You can get your phone to make calls, check the weather forecast, schedule a calendar appointment, or set a reminder. If you're happy to do this, a lot of things can be done in an otherwise wasted space of time: whilst you are driving.

9. Cleaning robot

This is pure magic! The one we have at home is one that has two functions: dry mop, and wet mop. I still marvel at the amount of dust, fluff, hair, and dirt this little thing can pick up, even though I've owned it for years!

It didn't come cheap, but I adore it because I can switch it on in a room in the house before we leave in the morning, and come back to find a clean floor. I usually put it right back to work in another room as soon as I arrive home, recharge the battery, and put it on again in the evening. There are a couple of cheaper options, but I do recommend reading reviews before going ahead and buying.

The services

1. Cleaner

Whilst costing quite a bit of money, the return on investment here is phenomenal.

Think about how much time you can save.

What takes a cleaner five hours can very easily take you double unless you are cleaning whilst everyone is asleep. Try one out for a month and you will be amazed at how much time and mental energy you will free up! If you use an agency or find someone you can trust, give the cleaner a spare set of keys (or drop them off that morning if possible) and allow them to do their work whilst you are at work too. That way, they can get their work done comfortably, and you can come home to a clean house.

2. Ironing services

Some cleaners also iron, but if not, there are specific ironing services available. These companies, or individuals, are very good at picking up your laundry, getting it ironed, and delivering it back to you. Most charge by the hour.

3. Internet banking

If you haven't signed up for it already, do so as soon as possible. This is a free service that will save you so much time driving to the bank and queuing, and not just that—you are also able to pay multiple payees and bills.

Any questions or queries can easily be handled online, as well as making it possible for you to closely monitor your credit cards and debit cards.

4. Delivery services

If you can get it delivered, do so! From groceries, to detergents, gas, or gifts—getting your shopping delivered is so convenient! Most of the time, deliveries are free of charge too provided you spend a minimum amount. Consider teaming up with colleagues to make sure you spend the minimum amount and get products delivered to your workplace. You can also do this with neighbours, or family and friends that live close by.

KEY POINTS

1. If possible, invest in products and services that will save you time.

2. Remember that whilst money comes and goes, time cannot be bought.

Products to consider

☐ Large freezer
☐ Tumble dryer
☐ Dishwasher
☐ Microwave
☐ Slow cooker
☐ Vacuum cleaner
☐ Voice-activated hands-free kit
☐ Cleaning robot

Services to consider

☐ Cleaner
☐ Ironing services
☐ Internet banking
☐ Delivery services

CHAPTER 2
HOME IS WHERE THE HEART IS

"A place for everything, and everything in its place."
—Mrs Beeton
(The Book of Household Management)

PREPARATION WORK

You *must* have a place for everything. Every. Little. Thing. The highlighter pens, the spare towels, the little extra buttons that come attached to new clothes, the padlocks you use once a year to lock your suitcases when you travel...you name it.

Luckily for me, we moved house a few years ago and, being the organised freak that I am, I spent hours agonising over where every little thing should go. I literally drove my husband up the wall brainstorming storage spaces and nooks and crannies for specific items. Looking back, he is thankful I took the time to think about all that, as our house is super-organised and everything has its own storage space.

If you are moving to a new home or renovating, reflect on ways you can integrate more storage solutions into your house. Before opting for a large house, ask yourself if the size is larger than you can handle in terms of cleaning and upkeep, and be aware of furniture or tiles that are a nightmare to keep clean. Glossy surfaces, or intricate designs usually require more attention.

Room by room organisation strategies

The entryway

If you do not have an entryway, allocate a designated space as close to the door as possible for putting away keys, and incoming and outgoing mail. It may be just a little shelf or drawer. All we have at home is a pretty box on the wall unit next to the front door for our keys, and a small cupboard for mail, and bits and pieces going in and out of the house.

There's nothing quite as messy or unhygienic as sets of keys on the kitchen counters, and having your keys placed in the same place every day can save you ample time searching high and low for them each morning. Wherever your keys are placed, they should not be within reach of younger children. Cheeky toddlers love indulging in a little 'hide and seek' with mum's or dad's keys!

If your space is larger, you can use an area to put away things which have just come home and need to be stored away, or things which need to leave the house. You may call this your transition space. Items such as library books, clothing items that need to be returned to a store, school application forms, or shopping parcels can be stowed away until they are ready to be taken in or out of your home.

> *"For every minute spent organising, an hour is earned."*
> — Benjamin Franklin

Bathroom

- Install magnetic strips on the inside of your medicine cabinet and hang tweezers, nail clippers, nail files, and scissors.

- Organise your medicine into separate boxes for separate uses, for example, kids, pain relief, stomach medication, and miscellaneous. Use what works for you. Check these on a regular basis and throw out any expired medicine immediately. I like to do this every time I buy something new, so it is a short and regular exercise.

- Use drawer organisers or utensil separators to save yourself time and grief hunting for bobby pins, hairbands, cotton discs, and every other itty bitty thing.

- Buy an over-the-door hanger to hang towels or bathrobes. Bath towels take up so much space and are easily stored and accessed by being hung.

- Invest in ultra large towels to throw over the floor to minimise water messes. Whether you have a walk-in shower, bathtub with a curtain, or a closed shower, it's easy to end up with water all over the floor every time someone has a bath or shower (especially little someones). Once that person is done the towel can be removed and— tada—dry, clean floors!

Kitchen

- Store your herbs and spices in small lidless boxes that fit in nicely into a designated drawer or pull-out cupboard or shelf. Write the name of the particular herb in felt tip pen on each and every herb's lid. This makes looking for herbs and spices a breeze. Just a quick glance does the trick.

- Place items you use on a daily basis in the most convenient places, and items which you use less often in harder to reach cupboards.

- If you have a larder, store, or floor-to-ceiling cabinetry, buy extra of the most used, hardest to find, or on offer food items or detergents. Keep one or two of each on hand in the lower cupboards and the extra ones in the very top or less accessible cabinets or spaces.

- Keep your kitchen tools on hand by storing them in a pretty container.

- Make use of the inside of your cupboard. Affix an over-the-door organiser to the inside of the door for bits and pieces, or a magazine holder which can hold foil, baking paper, garbage bags, and such.

- Sacrifice a deep drawer for vegetable storage. Get a skilled carpenter to insert a wire mesh in place of the front part of the drawer.

- Invest in glass water bottles. They're as cheap as chips and look great. Glass is better for the environment!

- Conceal rubbish bins if possible. I searched high and low for three bins with the perfect size to fit into the deep drawer beneath the sink: one for general waste, one for recyclables, and one for biodegradable waste.

- Clean out the fridge on a weekly basis, possibly the day on or before your weekly shopping is taken care of. Check expiry dates and put the items with the closest expiry dates at the front.

- One shelf in the fridge should be dedicated to ready-to-eat food: leftover chicken, extra quinoa, or snacks and lunches at the ready.

- Store healthy 'to go' snacks for the kids in a drawer where they can all easily reach and sift through.

Bedroom & closet

- Under-bed storage is a lifesaver. I utilise this space to store my handbags. There are several types of under-bed storage, the most accessible being drawers. We opted for this type of storage by purchasing a bed with a deep base with two drawers on each side of the bed. If you have a standard bed you can always buy under-bed storage containers. There are also beds with storage which is accessible by hoisting up the bed base which would have a specific mechanism for this purpose installed. This is terrific for space, but somehow inconvenient if you would like to take something out of storage if there is someone on the bed. It is a little harder to manage than just opening a drawer, although it may be used for less-used items like off-season clothing, bed sheets, and Christmas decorations.

- Just like floor-to-ceiling cabinets are a must in the kitchen, the same goes for wardrobes. Off-season or less used items may go on the top shelves. Vacuum bags are great for pieces which do not crease or are more forgiving, such as winter sheets and blankets, thermals, and such.

> *"How many things are there which I do not want"*
> —Socrates

- Less is definitely more when it comes to your closet! Only buy, keep, and wear things which you love and make you feel amazing!

- Give away any unwanted items which are in good condition to charity.

- Any clothing items needing hemming, buttons, or such should be placed in a bag and taken care of as soon as possible. Put them into your 'transition space' or in your car and schedule a drop off in your diary to whoever is doing it for you if you are unable to do it yourself.

- How many times do you come across a clothing item which you do not wear anymore but for some reason or other you feel you cannot part with? Place all these items in a bag, close it up, and deposit it somewhere where you can forget about it for a month. Set a reminder on your phone for 30 days later. If you cannot remember what is in the bag, do not open it and take it straight to your nearest charity. Works like a charm every time!

- Organise clothes by type (skirt, shirt, jacket) or by colour. By type works better as colour stands out but looking for a pair of classic trousers will be quite a feat if you need to look in every colour section in your wardrobe!

- Hang your whites inside out to keep them looking pristine.

- Too many pairs of tights? Use a couple of shoe boxes to store them by colour. Knot them into separate pieces to avoid ending up with a tangled mess.

- Small nightstand? Install a wall light and save precious space.

- Jewellery can be a headache to store. Buy drawer separators to keep your chunkier bracelets apart from your necklaces, and so forth. Buy small, transparent, fabric bags from eBay to store each piece of jewellery separately. Daintier pieces can fit nicely in a jewellery box.

- Fold linen neatly and use one of the pillowcases as a storage bag for the rest of the set. No more hunting for that pink pillowcase which seems to go AWOL every darn time.

Kids' bedroom

- Installing a magnetic noticeboard in the older children's room is a great brainwave! You can hang an 'easy snack list' which they are able to prepare themselves, their morning to-do list, and other important reminders.

- Buy a couple of stylish shoebox-type boxes to store bits and pieces. They're perfect for stationery! If you do not have a home office, you can display these pretty boxes on the shelves in the kids' bedrooms. IKEA has a range of pretty ones costing next to nothing. They are ideal for pens, staplers, tape, labels, copybooks and copybook covers, paper clips, rubbers, rulers, sharpeners, and so on! Always buy extra stationery consumables and keep them in these boxes—school-aged children go through pencils and rubbers like crazy!

- Install hooks behind the door—the larger the better. Hang bags (lunch, sport), the next day's uniform or outfit, and anything you want to keep off the floor! They're also extremely handy to keep clothes off the chairs and beds; if your kids can't reach the top section of the wardrobe they can use these hooks—no excuses! Works wonders for teaching younger kids to keep their room tidy, and to hang up clean clothes if the wardrobe is still out of reach!

- For younger kids, storage containers work a treat. I love IKEA's storage furniture with drawer type containers. You can opt for different colours and sizes. Teach your kids to put away their toys into the right container. This makes for easier playtimes—no more missing pieces!

- Find a small nook such as a small drawer or even a bag (this can be hung on the top hooks installed behind the door) to put away any clothes the kids grow out of. This happens at such an alarmingly fast rate that it's easy to end up with a large pile before you know it! Whether you are keeping the items for younger kids, donating, or selling, get rid of the bag as soon as it's full.

- Give your kids their own laundry basket for their bedroom.

- Assign a junk drawer and assist or ask for it to be cleaned out every month.

DAILY TO-DO'S

Chances are, most of the things on your daily to-do list start getting crossed off after your youngest children go to bed.

That said, there are a few tasks which can be done whilst you spend quality time with your little ones. What's very effective (and endearing!) is to include the children in some chores. This is mostly for younger children, aged one to five. My favourites are 'sort the laundry,' which can be turned into a colour sorting game; 'clean up,' which involves clearing up toys whilst singing; and 'the ten-minute dash' during which we turn on a timer and give the house a quick makeover.

EFFICIENCY TIP

The breakfast counter serves as a great place to serve snacks to the kids whilst you chat away about your day and get some food prep in. Get them involved by handing them a plastic knife and a chopping board. They will learn to help, cook, and will be enticed to try out new foods.

Working on your agenda

Once your children are getting their z's, you can start working your way down your list. Feel free to make an actual list and to then triumphantly tick off your accomplishments. There's more than one advantage to this:

1. You will not forget anything.

2. Putting everything down is a relief in itself; no more nagging thoughts in your head.

3. If your hubby, mum, best friend, or older child wants to pitch in, a quick reference is at hand.

4. It feels so satisfying to tick off what's done one by one as you work your way down a list!

Your list can be digital; you can use an app on your smartphone or tablet, or you can buy a pretty notebook or two and use it to jot down your to-do's.

EFFICIENCY TIP

Start from the things low on your priority list first. The later it gets, and the more tired you become, the more likely you are to shrug off something or other as your energy levels start dwindling. Leaving the most important items till the end is an easy hack you can use to make sure everything gets done!

Your ideal evening to-do list

1. Choose and lay out or hang the next day's outfit, including underwear, accessories, handbag and shoes. Iron anything which needs to be ironed.

2. Prepare kids uniforms. Clean their shoes and prepare them next to the door along with their jackets.

3. Check schoolbags for any papers that need to be signed and sent back. In the case of younger children, check their communication book to see if there is any stationery which needs to be bought, or any homework to be made.

4. Prep for breakfast.

5. Prepare for the next day's dinner and the day after, if possible. If anything needs to be taken out of the freezer, plan to do it on time so that your food can thaw slowly in the fridge.

6. Prepare lunches for everyone for the following day, or

making ahead if possible.

7. Go through the house for a quick clean-up.

8. Clean the kitchen.

ORGANISATION TIP

Simple tasks which can be done by any family member, such as loading or unloading the dishwasher, clearing the house, or putting toys back in their place should always be left for last. When another family member is able to pitch in, make sure there is something for them to do! Better yet, assign tasks to different members of the family.

TASK SHARING FOR ALL THE FAMILY

What makes time management successful is sharing of tasks in the household. Everyone lives in your home, and likewise everyone needs to pull their socks up and help. Do not feel like it is your job; everyone is responsible. Granted, you might still need to oversee everything and probably pitch in some more, especially if you spend the most time at home, but make no excuses for the rest of the family.

Kids can pitch in according to their age, whilst other home chores must also be shared between all the adult members of the household. Always take into consideration the amount of time each individual actually spends at home for a fair distribution of household responsibilities. Also keep in mind everybody's strengths and weaknesses. Whilst I am a whiz at budgeting, I cannot iron if my life depended on it. My husband, on the other hand, is very patient and capable in this department and does not mind ironing on Sunday nights whilst watching his favourite series.

Home chores - How, when, and who

There is more to be done in the home than the eye can see. Read this list and then assign tasks accordingly. Add or remove items on the list as you see fit. Some of the chores would need to be left out or done less frequently if you have a maid or housekeeper.

HOUSEWORK

____ Making beds
____ Washing dishes/loading & unloading dishwasher
____ Taking out the trash
____ Watering plants
____ Laundry

CLEANING

____ Sweeping & vacuuming
____ Cleaning windows & mirrors
____ Wiping down furniture & washing floors
____ Washing cars
____ Daily light cleaning of kitchen & toilets

_____ Seasonal cleaning of soft furnishings

FOOD

_____ Cooking

_____ Preparing work/school lunches

_____ Attending to fridges and freezers (knowing what's inside, removing spoilt items, keeping them clean & organised)

_____ Grocery shopping & other errands

ORGANISING TASKS

_____ Preparing menu plans & shopping lists

_____ Daily organising of the house

_____ Clearing out & organisation of wardrobes

_____ Managing appointments

MISCELLANEOUS

_____ Servicing of air conditioners & other appliances

_____ Paying bills & filing of paperwork

_____ Money management

_____ Feeding pets

_____ Buying cards & presents

_____ Booking holidays

_____ Organising birthday parties & events

KIDS

____ Kids & morning routine

____ Liaising with school/nursery

____ Kids' extracurricular activity management

____ Helping kids with homework & school matters

____ Getting the kids to school

____ Kids' bedtime routines

____ Kids' bath times

____ _____

____ _____

____ _____

____ _____

____ _____

____ _____

Getting the kids to pitch in

You would be surprised how helpful the kids can be. Start them off from a young age, so that chores form a part of their everyday family life.

Here are some do's and don'ts:

DO make chores fun! Switch on the music and dance whilst you and the kids are busy or play 'basketball' with dirty clothes as you throw them in the laundry basket.

DON'T complain about your chores! Cleaning the bathroom *is* a mundane task after a full-on day at the office and at home, but if you feel like complaining, do not do it in front of your kids. If that is the attitude you exude, do you blame them for complaining? Instead, put on a bright smile and thank the stars that you have the energy to do all that!

DO offer praise. Children enjoy feeling appreciated. Take a moment to tell your child specifically *why* they did such a good job.

DON'T redo a chore. As messy as the bed may look, if your three-year-old made an effort to make his or her own bed, do not under any circumstances remake it for it to look perfect! Doing so would only send out the message: "You are not good enough!"

DO use a chore chart. Nothing spells motivation like a good old chore chart. Make it easy to use, and tie it in with an incentive upon the completion of all the weekly chores. Some agree with tying in an allowance upon the completion of chores, and some do not.

DON'T use chores as a punishment. Nothing can be more negative than doing so. Your child will associate chores with punishment and will definitely deem them as something negative. Can you blame them?

DO teach your kids how to get dressed from as an early an age as possible. It is such a blessing for them to be able to do it on their own while you can get breakfast ready or get some things sorted around the house. You might get the odd sweater put on back to front, but most of the time it's fine, and mornings are so much easier on everyone.

DON'T give them too much to do. With school, studying, homework, and extra curricular activities, you need to allow for some down time for your little ones. Aim for an hour of chores during the weekend during school months, and add more responsibilities during the summer.

DO make up little games to make housework more fun! A sure-fire way to get everyone to sort out the house quickly is to play 'beat the clock'. Set a timer for ten minutes and get the kids to clear their bedrooms very quickly and get their toys out of the way. First person to finish, wins!

Tasks for kids by age

Ages 2-3

Helping in making their bed
Picking up and putting away toys
Helping to sort laundry
Cleaning up their spills/messes
Wiping furniture (height restrictions apply, of course!)
Helping to empty shopping bags

Ages 4-5

All of the above, plus:
Emptying waste paper baskets
Bringing in any mail
Feeding any small pets
Fixing a bowl of cereal
Helping to unload the dishwasher
Getting dressed
Making their own drinks

Ages 6-8

All of the above, plus:
Taking out the recycling
Folding towels
Watering plants
Sweeping floors
Fixing simple snacks

Ages 9-11

All of the above, plus:
Cleaning toilets
Taking out the trash
Cooking very basic meals
Folding & putting away laundry

Ages 12+

All of the above, plus:
Walking pets
Watching younger siblings
Mopping floors
Cooking a meal

KEEPING YOUR HOME ORGANISED & CLUTTER-FREE

"Have nothing in your house that you do not know to be useful, or believe to be beautiful."
—William Morris

Organisation and decluttering are two very different things. Whilst most people think that they are the most disorganised beings on the planet, the actual issue might be that they are not decluttering.

ORGANISATION TIP

Decluttering is more important than organisation and is very often underestimated. We feel we need to be more organised but what we actually need is to own less.

Decluttering your home makes the house instantly look cleaner. It is also so much easier to clean when you own less and have no bits and pieces lying around waiting to be picked up or moved on. Seeking to own less to free up space is a gratifying experience.

Having an organised and clutter-free home starts with choosing what goes into your home. You do not need to be a minimalist to reap the fruits of a junk-free home.

Quick tips for avoiding and getting rid of clutter

1. When buying items for your home, choose wisely. Only buy items that you love and need; do not shop on a whim.

2. Limit yourself. Stick to the laws of physics. If there is absolutely *no way* you can have more than eight coffee mugs on that shelf, stick to eight coffee mugs. Buy eight very pretty, matching mugs and give away any other that come your way.

3. The 'one in, one out' rule works a treat. For every item that comes into your house, a similar item must go. Your

home can only hold so many of the same thing—so hold on to your favourites and part with the rest.

4. Do not get emotionally attached to objects. If you find yourself saying, "What if I need it?" or "One day I could use this for...", or "I might need this when...", you are clearly stuck and need to take yourself out of the situation to assess if you truly need what you're desperately trying to hang on to.

5. Get a 'power hour' in. Gretchin Rubin, who wrote several books about happiness and good habits, swears by this. Once a week, for one hour, deal with nagging tasks or chores. Why not fit in your own 'power hour' into your schedule and get decluttering? Try it! You would be surprised with what you can get done in an hour!

6. Give away to family, friends, or thrift stores. Think of your less-used or liked things going to someone who needs them.

7. Learn that having less is more (more of what you need and love!), and enjoy the peace it brings with it.

Kids & toys

There are so many toys on offer, and being mamas who love our kids to bits, understandably, we all struggle with limiting toys. After all, what's more loving than gifting our children and giving them lots of toys to make them happy?

Because of this very same loving gesture we end up having toys strewn everywhere and waste so much time trying to look for missing bits and bobs. Even worse, when company drops by unexpectedly, we end up frantically shoving toys into closets and baskets to try to make the house look halfway decent!

Easy ways to limit toys

- Convince yourself that your kids don't need so much 'stuff' to keep them happy. Think back to when you were little. Do your fondest memories involve toys? If they do, was it a specific toy, or a whole load of them?

- Teach your children boundaries from an early age. Allocate a space for their toys. Show them the space and explain that that is the toys' home and that they cannot have more toys than what fits in this allocated space. If their space is full, and they would like to have something else, ask them if there is anything they are not using and can give away.

- Any unused toys may be given away to friends or charity. Involve your child in the process. They will learn the value of giving.

- Teach your children to declutter by explaining why they need to do it. You can gently say:

  "You know what, your bedroom needs to be cleared out. You have so many toys you do not use. Let's go through them and see what you don't play with any more so we may give them to kids who are not as lucky to have so many toys as you. Let's keep your favourites. What do you think?"

If kids are treated like young adults, they are so much more receptive, and this sets a great example.

- Use the 'black bag' method. If a child is unsure of whether he or she wants to give away something, you can say:

  "I can see that you are not sure and feeling unhappy that you need to decide if this toy needs to stay or go. Let's put it into this black bag and store it in the box room for a while. If you decide you want it back at any point in time just say so to mummy and I will give it back to you. If you do not need it, however, and it stays there, that would mean that you do not need it any longer, so we will give it away. Does that work for you?"

- Give 'toy rotation' a shot. After discarding any unwanted, unused, broken, or incomplete toys, take out all your child's toys and divide into three categories—Thinking toys: puzzles, Legos, etc; Action toys: balls, cars, etc; and Pretend toys: dolls, toy food sets, dress-up, etc. Fill up as many boxes as you wish with a limited mixture from all the three categories. Allow your child one box of toys; the rest may be displayed lovingly on bedroom shelves and pretty baskets. Every two to three weeks (you decide) put away all the toys and rotate with another box.

Enjoy the process of learning together and teach your kids to be adults. Teach them to choose and buy wisely, to store intelligently, and to take care of their belongings.

HOUSEWORK

LAUNDRY

Laundry day vs one load a day

Do you have a laundry day, do you handle one load every day or every other day, or do you do a load of laundry whenever you feel the need to do one?

Unless you work from home or want to spend one day out of your precious two-day weekend at home doing the laundry, laundry day does not really make much sense.

EFFICIENCY TIP

One load a day (or every other day) is practical and easy if you take a few simple steps to prepare in the morning. If you do not plan for it in the morning, it can be very difficult to get the loads done on time and can drag on into late evening when all you should be doing is sitting down with a cuppa.

Don't feel overwhelmed. Follow these simple instructions to get it done in no time!

1. Every morning, separate your dirty laundry and gather the clothes you will be washing. Place them in the washing

machine and put the detergent in. If you have a delay timer, time your washing machine to be ready round about the time you get home. If your washing machine does not come with a delay timer, buy a smart plug which has a Wi-Fi connection and start your washing machine from wherever you are using your smartphone.

2. Once you get home, your clothes are washed. In they go into the tumble dryer. If you have a washer/dryer, your clothes are already dry.

3. Get your clothes out of the tumble drier as soon as they are ready, to avoid creasing. If you are in the middle of something else, quickly take them out and lay them flat on chairs or a bed to wait for you.

4. At the end of your day, the last thing you feel like doing is folding your laundry. Sit down and enjoy watching television while you fold them. Time will fly, and you will be ready before you know it!

Quick tips for laundry

• Pre-sorting your dirty laundry into colours saves you five to ten minutes each morning. Buying a laundry basket with separate sections for pre-sorting will help you sort on the spot. Teach your kids to pre-sort their clothes, and if possible, have hampers in their room just in case they get the colours mixed up.

• Wash clothes with cold water unless you're washing workout clothes or really dirty, muddy clothes, or bed linens. Hot water kills germs but is not otherwise very ideal. Hot water can damage fabrics, make colours run, and can shrink some fabric types. If you have stains in your clothes, hot water is your enemy. Contrary to popular belief, hot water *sets* stains. If you want to get stains out, wash in cold water. Cold water is also fine for most clothes, plus it's environmentally friendly.

- Stain hack alert! Whenever you need to get a stain out, use dishwashing soap and cold water. Try to get it out as soon as possible, but even if not, this has had a brilliant 95% success rate for me. No more being overwhelmed with stain removal 'solutions'!

- Invest in an iron steam station. It costs a little more than your traditional iron and is a tad bulkier, but ironing time is cut down drastically, at least by 50-60%!

If your kids are aged 13 and over they are perfectly capable of doing their own laundry, or of helping with a load or two. Consider adding this as a summer chore. It's a fantastic life skill to teach your children!

CLEANING

Keeping your house clean (ha!)

Granted, we're all able to clean up messes and wash the floors, but what if we were to take some small steps to actually keep the house in a clean state so there is less to clean up? Having a maid that comes to your home once a week to clean top to bottom is wonderful. If you can manage to keep your home as clean as possible in between the maid's weekly visits, all you need to do throughout the week is minimal cleaning.

Some basic changes can go a long way in keeping your home clean:

- My number one rule for keeping a home clean is not to wear shoes inside the house. Besides bringing in dust, mud, and leaving unsightly footprints on your floors, numerous germs and bacteria are also brought into your home.

- If you have shower doors, keep a small squeegee in the bathroom and use it every time you shower.

- If you notice a spill or a few water splashes, clean up straight away. Use paper towels for water or a cloth and some soap to spot clean.

- When frying, cover the pan with a splatter screen to avoid having oil droplets splattered all over your floors or countertops.

- Keep a bag on the kitchen counter to throw away scraps while you cook. Avoiding coming and going to the dustbin not only helps you avoid making a mess, but saves you time. I like to reuse bags in which food was packaged in, such as cereal or frozen foods.

- Clean as you cook, and clean the kitchen after every meal.

- Use the 'one-minute rule'. If anything can be done in under a minute, do it straight away. Don't put your glass in the sink, but rinse, dry, and put it away immediately. Hang your jacket in your closet as you walk through the door.

- Always look around you as you move from room to room. Never leave a room empty-handed, always take something which needs to be placed in the room you are going to.

- Put old newspaper at the bottom of your trash can to soak up any food juices.

EFFICIENCY TIP

Educate your children to clean up their own spills and messes from a very young age. Even if not entirely successful, they will come a long way in the years to come. Ask everyone to pitch in in their own little way, even if it is just a simple wipe of the table after dinner.

How to clean if...

You have a cleaner who comes once a week:

Only do the absolute basic daily necessities like cleaning the kitchen, toilets and sinks, sweeping or vacuuming, and spot cleaning.

If you have a cleaner who comes every fortnight:

Besides doing the basic daily necessities mentioned above, dedicate a couple of hours a week (depending on the size of your home) to wipe down furniture and wash the floors of high traffic areas.

If you do not have a cleaner:

You can either have a cleaning day or else can clean a little every day. This strongly depends on your lifestyle and personal situation. If you do opt for a cleaning day, combining it with laundry day is a good option.

In any case, I use my cleaning robot on a daily basis. It is switched on twice a day on rotation, particularly in the kitchen and living area and in the bedrooms. I only ever use my broom to clear up messes!

DAILY CLEANING QUICK TIPS

The toilets

1. Generously drop in toilet bowl cleaner and let it sit for a while.

2. Spray a sanitising cleaner onto the toilet rim and seat.

3. Give the countertops a quick wipe down.

4. Spray some bathroom cleaner into the sink and wipe.

5. Wipe down the toilet using paper towels—easier to manage as you can discard right after use, and more hygienic too.

6. Clean the toilet bowl using the toilet brush.

The kitchen

1. Whilst still sitting at the table, clear the plates by emptying the waste into one plate. Wipe clean with the used napkins. Wiped plates and cutlery go into a neat stack, whilst one plate carries the waste.

2. Everyone in the family can lend a hand by taking something to the kitchen. Little kids can carry non-breakables such as the napkins. Place all the dirty plates in a designated area next to the sink or dishwasher.

3. Wipe down the kitchen table.

4. Clear the kitchen counters and throw away any waste into the bag on your counter.

5. Wipe down kitchen countertops.

6. If you have a dishwasher, load it.

7. Hand wash dishes which do not go into the dishwasher or all the dishes if you do not have one. Start with smaller items first, so that you may place the larger items on top.

8. Leave the plates out to dry naturally. They can easily be put away in the morning or last thing before you go to bed.

KEY POINTS

1. Having a designated space for all your belongings is the mother of organisation.

2. Involve family members in household chores by turning chores into games and by assigning suitable tasks for each member.

3. The value of decluttering is often underestimated. A good decluttering session will instantly breathe life into your space.

4. Kids do not need tons of toys to keep them happy. Less is definitely more in the toy department.

5. Implementing a few strategic steps will help you avoid overwhelm when trying to deal with your laundry.

6. A few simple basic changes will do wonders towards keeping your house clean.

CHAPTER 3
FOR THE LOVE OF FOOD

"There is no love sincerer than the love of food."
—George Bernard Shaw
(Man and Superman)

PROPER PLANNING IS 90% OF THE WORK

Meal prep with decent hearty food is one of the most time and energy consuming chores out of all the chores that need to be taken care of.

You can obviously take shortcuts and buy lunch everyday whilst at work, and have the kids eat school-prepared lunches or at the school cafeteria but can you stomach (pun intended) all the processed, unhealthy food on a daily basis? Not only that, but your bank account will also thank you if you opt for homemade lunches! Resort to ready-made lunch on the busiest of days, or during emergencies.

A little thought can go a long way in the food department. I do suggest you focus most of your energy on dinnertime since it is usually the meal where the family sits together. If your lifestyle does not adapt well to this, consider focusing more on a time that is more convenient for your family, such as breakfast.

Meal Planning

ORGANISATION TIP

One option is to plan for the following week. Look at your calendar and jot down the dinner recipes for each day according to the appointments or plans you have for that particular day. A structure of sorts for the week will help you flow through the days without hesitation.

Another option is to pre-plan the month ahead by picking recipes for the entire month. You might think this is overly exhausting but in actual fact, this will save you a lot of time. It has the added advantage that you can really look at your month at a glance and make sure you are including enough veggies, proteins, and healthy food all month long.

Plan a shopping list for the chosen recipes. Personally, I like to split mine into four (one a week), for reasons of storage space, freshness, and any last minute change of plans.

EFFICIENCY TIP

If you are a family of four, you can easily cook four portions in a slow cooker and have one portion once a week, each week. That works out brilliantly because you can get most of your cooking done in one week!

This plan works a treat with family favourites. Plan to batch cook as many portions as possible in your slow cooker, and eat the meal on rotation once a week.

A little extra can be put aside and popped in the freezer as a backup. If you love experimenting in the kitchen, or if you have picky eaters, these backup portions will be put to good use if your kids do not like what you've put on the table. I'm not one to cook separate meals for the kids and us, but I am realistic; I don't expect my children to like something exotic that I would have wanted to try!

Quick tips for food planning & meal prep

1. Keep your eyes and ears open for ideas

If someone is raving about a recipe ask them to send you the link. Sharing your favourite recipes with co-workers will inspire them to do the same!

2. Never cook just one portion per person

Once you are taking the time to plan, buy, chop, prep, and cook, you might as well cook in bulk and freeze. Take note of by how many times you are multiplying a recipe. Specific pans fit specific amounts of ingredients for different recipes. If you are saving the recipes digitally, make a note in the file name (x2, or x3, or x4). If the recipe is being cooked in your slow cooker, I'd also advise writing the cooking time and heat setting, especially if the timing was perfect. If not, still take note and also note if the food was on the dry side or slightly undercooked, for easy reference next time round.

3. Try to choose dishes which may be frozen

If not, find ways to use extra portions in different ways. Take, for example, chicken salad. Day 1: Chicken salad; Day 2: Chicken salad side plate; Day 3: Red peppers stuffed with chicken salad. The chicken leftovers may also be used for lunch, in a sandwich or wrap.

4. Experiment, but do not choose anything too complicated...

...or time consuming unless it is the weekend or a quiet night and you are cooking to relax. We are so spoilt for choice today and options are limitless.

5. If you do not like a recipe, delete it...

...or rid yourself of the printout straight away. Avoid having a lot of recipes cluttering your devices and files.

6. Be systematic

Try a new recipe and then keep it or toss it. This will make it easier for you to find and repeat the recipes you loved.

PLANNING AHEAD

Once you have picked your recipes, it's time to create your shopping lists.

There are several ways to do this.

One of the most effective methods is to use a shared grocery list app, one which you can use on several devices and share with a member of your household. Once you enter any item into any specific shopping list, say 'milk' in the 'supermarket' list, this may be viewed across devices.

Let's say your partner goes to the supermarket to shop and accesses the list. They may cross out the items on the list which in turn may be viewed by you in real time. It is uber-cool to open up the app and watch the list of groceries disappear one by one—I always know if my husband is ready from his errand or if he has just arrived at the supermarket!

Of course, if you are the paper and pen type of person, go for it! Digital lists are not for everyone! Keep a small notebook for your lists which you can shuffle between handbags and kitchen counters. The downside to using pen and paper is that you cannot share these lists as easily with anyone else as you can do with the digital version; however, you can cheat—snap a photo of your list and send it to the kind-hearted soul picking up a few things for you from the grocery store!

ORGANISATION TIP

Try and be well prepared so as not to run out of anything specific and have to rush to the store to buy one or two items.

It is such a hassle and a complete time-waster to do so. If you do decide to go for the digital app list, which I totally recommend, take note of anything that runs out the second it does. The lovely thing about these apps is that you can have several separate shopping lists such as 'pharmacy', 'school supplies', 'supermarket', and so on.

Using the freezer

It's surprising how many foods freeze well. Always keep a spare of each of the following in your freezer for emergencies (subject to what you consume, of course), and freeze any extra amounts as soon as possible before they start to spoil.

Bread

Super easy to freeze, anything goes!

Milk

Freeze it in its carton and let it thaw slowly in the fridge when required.

Cheese

All cheeses may be frozen, but the firmer varieties freeze better. This is not to say that softer cheeses cannot be frozen, but the texture may change slightly.

Eggs

This is the most surprising of them all! Crack the eggs and freeze them in separate small ziplock bags or an ice cube tray. They may be frozen for up to a year.

Yoghurt

Just pop it in the freezer; delicious if eaten frozen!

Garlic

They may be frozen whole (garlic is so much more easily

chopped from frozen!), or peeled and chopped.

Avocados

You need to wash, cut, and peel it, remove the stone, and put it in a ziplock bag. The texture will change slightly but the avocado will make for a great smoothie or guacamole.

Shopping

Online shopping is a great option if you have babies, multiples, a large family, little or no help, or children with challenging behaviour.

There are many perks to online grocery shopping, including:

1. You are able to save your weekly shopping list on the specific online shop's website and don't need to input the items you buy each and every time, such as milk, water, bread etc.

2. It can be done at your own time and in the comfort of your own home.

3. The delivery people bring the bags straight to your door, and most often, to your kitchen.

4. The food arrives in perfect condition;frozen food stays frozen since it is delivered in a refrigerated vehicle.

5. Avoiding crowds, queues, and traffic.

There are a few disadvantages worth mentioning, including the following:

1. You have no control over quality, freshness, and expiry dates.

2. You do not have the option to select your own fruit or make sure cans are not dented.

3. Not every store you enjoy buying from has an online shop.

Quick tips for supermarket visits

- If you can manage to get someone else to make the supermarket trip, hurrah! Whoever is going, it's best to visit on Tuesday, Wednesday, or Thursday evenings, as that's when supermarkets are the quietest.

- If you are going with your kids, try to go at a time when they are well-rested and fed.

- Cheat a little and take a sneaky snack that is usually a one-off occasion, or a toy that they have not used for a while and leave these in your bag in case all hell breaks loose.

- If your child is going through a phase of being supremely grumpy, and it is physically impossible to manage them and a shopping list, plus a shopping cart, write your shopping list on sticky notes. As soon as you get to the supermarket stick the labels on the trolley handle. It really saves you a ton of energy trying to refer to your list when you're desperately trying to keep your child entertained. My daughter passed through this difficult phase at about 16 months, and this tip saved me on several occasions!

- Use a cross-body bag instead of a handbag or backpack to free up your hands and be able to access it with ease.

- Get your kids involved. Ask them to help load the food into the trolley and turn it into a fun game.

- If your child won't sit in the trolley cart try one of two things: either get them to sit in the actual cart, and play peek-a-boo by having him or her hide amidst the groceries; or have them sit in their actual place and turn the cart around so that you are pushing from behind and they are facing forward.

- Last but not least, ignore the looks! You might get a few stares and judgmental looks from a few people if your toddler is screaming their head off because they want to go home. Don't worry about what might be running through people's heads—just remind yourself of what an amazing mama you are!

FAMILY FAVOURITES

EFFICIENCY TIP

Quick, healthy, freezable, slow cooked, portable (any two must apply!)

Breakfasts

The best breakfasts are definitely portable! Whether you do have time to sit down for breakfast, or not, portability ensures that breakfast is eaten on a daily basis. If your kids are rarely ever hungry in the morning, their breakfast can be eaten in the car or whilst waiting for the school bus.

Go-to breakfasts

EGG BAKES

A very easy and tasty egg casserole. Not only is this recipe high in protein but you can get most of your 5-a-day from it!

Makes 12 servings

Ingredients

6 eggs
2 handfuls spinach
250g provolone cheese
150g pancetta or ham cubes
1 tbsp parmesan
1 tsp chives
salt and pepper, to taste

Method

1. Combine eggs, spinach, provolone cheese, pancetta or ham cubes, parmesan, chives, and salt and pepper.
2. Pour into a dish lined with parchment paper.
3. Bake for about 25 minutes or until golden.

TOP TIP

This recipe is perfect to batch cook and freeze, and each portion will take up little room in the freezer. Freeze a week's worth of portions in one ziplock bag, and assuming you have taken the plunge and made at least two weeks' worth, take out one bag from the freezer every Sunday night and place in the fridge for an easy breakfast.

OVERNIGHT OATS IN A JAR

Slight prep work involved; however, you can prepare in advance and store for up to 5 days in the fridge.

Makes one serving

Ingredients

½ cup rolled oats
1 cup non–dairy milk such as almond or coconut
2 tbsp Greek yoghurt
1 tsp of honey
1 tsp almond butter
a handful of coconut flakes
half a banana
½ tsp chia seeds

Method

1. Combine the rolled oats, almond or coconut milk and the Greek yoghurt.
2. Add the honey, almond butter, coconut flakes, banana, and chia seeds.
3. Close the Mason jar and shake.
4. Keeps the oats in the fridge overnight.

TOP TIP

If all your family members have different tastes, prepare the basic recipe for 'overnight oats in a jar' and let everyone pick and choose their toppings each morning.

Simply combine the oats, milk and yoghurt and leave the rest up to everyone's individual tastes.

CHIA SEED PUDDING

Similar to overnight oats in a jar; however chia seed pudding is easier to make. It's very tasty and packed with fibre!

Makes one serving

Ingredients

3 cups non-dairy milk such as almond or coconut
½ cup chia seeds
2 tsp maple syrup or honey
For the topping:
fruit of your choice
nuts (optional)

Method

1. In a mason jar, mix the almond or coconut milk with the chia seeds.
2. Add the maple syrup or honey.
3. Add your desired topping
4. Place in the fridge for at least 1 to 2 hours.

You may store for up to 5 days

TOP TIP

This can also double as a great dessert - nutritious, impressive & easy to serve!

<u>SMOOTHIES</u>

1. Choose any fruit and/or vegetable combination. Chop, place in ziplock bags, and freeze in desired portions.
2. When you are up for a smoothie, take a bag out of the freezer, place in your hand blender container or otherwise, and blend.
3. Add your liquid base option: milk, non-dairy milk (coconut, almond, soy), coconut water, fruit juice, kefir, or cold tea or coffee.
4. *Optional. Add a thickener: oats, yoghurt flaxseed, chia seeds, or protein powder.*
5. *Dress it; also optional. Choose from: vanilla essence, almond (or any other nut) butter, avocado, nuts (pecans, cashews, hazelnut or any other).*

<u>TOP TIP</u>

Chop fruits and vegetables in bulk, pre-portion, and freeze individual servings in ziplock bags. When you would like to have a smoothie, take one out of the freezer and blend in your liquid base.

<u>BOILED EGGS</u>

The easiest of all.

<u>Method</u>

1. Boil a couple of eggs.
2. Peel them and let them cool.
3. Wrap them individually in foil and store them in the fridge.
    You can store them for up to seven days

Lunches

Look out for lunches which keep well for three to five days in the fridge, or if not, lunches that freeze well.

Instead of preparing lunches for each and every day, you might prefer to make extra dinner portions and have them for lunch the next day. I prefer to stick to a very simple recipe and prepare for a week's lunches on a Sunday evening. I generally put three day's worth in the fridge and freeze the rest.

These are a small sample of simple to prepare lunches which may be refrigerated or frozen:

QUINOA SALAD

Superduper easy, and you can make so many different variations!

- Quinoa can be frozen for up to 8 months.
- Double up on the veggies you are using for a particular recipe one night and add to your ready-made quinoa.
- A few favourite combos are tomato, mozzarella, pine nut & basil; shrimp, avocado, sweetcorn, red peppers & lime vinaigrette; feta, tomato, olive, cucumber & cilantro.

WRAPS (TORTILLAS)

Easy to prepare and so many fillings to choose from!

My favourite wrap combo is very easy to put together, and also very filling.

Makes 12 servings

Ingredients

1 tsp coconut oil
1 kg chicken breast, cut into strips
1 bag (500g) frozen vegetables (Asian or Mexican works well)
4 tbsp 'sauce' of your choice: barbecue, Mexican salsa, Greek yoghurt, or hummus are ideal)
5 wholegrain (large) 30cm wraps

Method

1. Add the coconut oil to a pan.
2. Pan fry the chicken breast in the pan until cooked well throughout.
3. Add your vegetables to the same pan.
4. Mix in your accompanying sauce, unless you have opted for hummus or Greek yoghurt.
5. Once your chicken and veg have cooked, remove from the hob and let the pan cool down slightly.
6. Cut out parchment paper (about 30 cm wide) and lay them on the kitchen counter.
7. Put your empty wraps over the parchment paper.
8. If you have opted for hummus or Greek yoghurt as your 'sauce', spread it on the wraps.

<u>Method - continued</u>

9. Distribute the chicken & vegetable mixture over the wraps and close them.
10. Wrap the wraps individually using the parchment paper.

The wraps should be frozen individually in parchment paper.

<u>TOP TIP</u>

When ready to devour, heat as is, in the parchment paper in the microwave for a minute. Transfer to a toaster (sandwich maker type) in the parchment paper to make for easy clean-up.

Wholegrain rice with chicken and veggies

The very same mixture used as wrap filling may be combined with wholegrain rice. You may prepare extra mixture, freeze it, and cook the rice when required.

Kids' lunches

Kids' lunches are another thing altogether. Considering that they need to be carried around in a lunchbox all day long, you have to be extra careful about what you pack, especially if you also happen to hail from a country with a very warm climate.

Bread

Although we try to limit bread, our kids love it, and coming

from a Mediterranean country we seem to thrive on carbo-
hydrates.

- Opt for healthier and more complex carbs such as
  wholegrain.

- Most bread, such as wholegrain bagels, freeze really well
  pre-prepared with your filling of choice. All you need to do
  in the morning is to take them out of the freezer and stick
  them into your child's lunchbox. By the time it's lunchtime
  the bagel would have thawed to a perfect temperature!

- A few filling ideas include: ham & cheese; tuna & mayo
  (cheat by using Greek yoghurt to make it healthier); chick-
  en & salad; and any other ingredient you are already combining with your 'adult' lunches.

Pasta salad

Again, wholegrain is best!

Feel free to use the same ingredients you are using for your
own lunches. That's one less thing to plan for! If your kids
enjoy a creamier 'mayo' texture, use Greek yoghurt; or at
most, go half and half with mayo. They will be none the wiser!

Wraps (Tortillas)

Besides making wraps for the adults, you can also prepare
smaller sized ones with the kids' favourite ingredients for their
lunches. Your little ones might enjoy eating them more if they
are made into 'pinwheels'.

How to prepare pinwheels:

1. Slather the wrap with a spread, such as hummus, cream cheese, Greek yoghurt, or tahini.

2. Lay the fillings on top.

3. Roll the wrap up tightly.

4. Cut up into bite-sized portions.

TIP: Refrigerate the rolled wrap for an hour or two before cutting up to help hold everything together.

Snacks for all

Pre-portioning food which can stay fresh for a couple of days in ziplock bags means that you always have snacks at the ready to be taken out of the cupboard or fridge at a moment's notice. This curbs a lot of 'Mum, I'm hungry' moments! This tip is also very helpful on weekends when it is such a feat to get the whole family out of the door but you have to pack some snacks to be nibbled on whilst you are running errands. This will save you a buck or two, and a couple of calories.

Here is a list of my favourite go-to snacks (suitable for both kids and adults alike, although some may appeal more to adults rather than the children):

•   Nuts

•   Crackers

•   Dried fruit

•   Cereal

- Fresh fruit - bananas and apples are the easiest to transport; just make sure that the apple is washed and that you always carry them in a bag which will then double as a garbage bag.

- Rice cakes

- Cereal and granola bars (very easy to make your own; look up some recipes!)

- Banana & oat cookies (so easy to make and such a favourite! Just combine 2 over-ripe bananas with 1 cup oats and mash to make a gooey mixture. Bake for 20 minutes and you're done! You can also add in dried fruit, nuts, chocolate chips—just use your imagination!)

- Seeds, such as sunflower and pumpkin

- Pretzels

- Yoghurt

Dinners

Once upon a time, you might have enjoyed cooking every day, with a glass of wine in one hand and background music playing softly.

Whilst some might still enjoy cooking, probably most of your daily dinners are more of a very-quickly-put-together kind of dinners.

Nutrition should still play an important part in dinner preparation, as should variety; however, simplicity usually beats anything else.

Most of my dinners are cooked in my slow cooker, which deserves a few pages of its own.

THE SLOW COOKER

My slow cooker remains my favourite appliance and method of cooking. It is the handiest kitchen tool and a must-have for saving time.

Quick tips for getting the most out of your slow cooker

- Prepare the ingredients for your recipe the night before, throw them into the slow cooker pot, and place it in the fridge.

- If your pot is made of clay, in the morning take it out of the fridge as early as possible and leave the pot out on the counter to give it time to come as close to room temperature as possible.

- If you are able to choose a multi cooker, even better. My slow cooker is also able to roast, bake, steam, and sauté—so many terrific features in one unit!

- You may opt to use slow cooker liners; however, these will add a significant cost to your dinners. In my humble opinion, this is an extra, and considering that the pot is dishwasher safe the extra cost if not justified.

- If you are new to your slow cooker, be warned that it takes some time getting used to. Get used to the pace at which your slow cooker cooks. You might get a couple of overdone risottos, dry chicken, and watery meals before you got the hang of it. Don't give up! Experiment. After a few tries you will learn how long to cook foods for and you will be able to adjust most recipes to be cooked in the slow cooker without having to follow a recipe.

A few slow cooker family favourites

PORK RIBS WITH HONEY GLAZE

This recipe is based on a 5.6-litre slow cooker, which fits 2 racks of ribs.

Makes 5 servings

Ingredients

2 racks of ribs
half a pint of beer
salt & pepper
For the glaze:
3 tbsp honey
2 tbsp brown sugar
1 tbsp dry English mustard
1 tbsp ketchup
1 tbsp wine vinegar

Method

1. Place the ribs vertically in your slow cooker.
2. Add the beer, and salt & pepper.

Method - continued

3. Cook for 6 hours on low.
4. Mix all the glaze ingredients in a small pot over low heat and stir until all the ingredients melt and blend.
5. When the ribs are cooked, open the slow cooker and let them cool.
6. Once cool, place the ribs on a grill rack covered with parchment paper and glaze them using half of the glaze.
7. Place under the grill for 15 minutes.
8. Glaze again with the remaining glaze and grill for a further 10 minutes or until golden on top.

TOP TIP

When the ribs are finished from their slow-cooking, give them time to cool before placing them on the grill rack. The slow cooking process literally makes the meat fall off the bones unless the ribs are cooled before being taken out of the slow cooker.

BEER CHICKEN

I love this recipe! Apart from being ridiculously easy, I freeze the chicken we do not eat into small ziplock bags and use them as filling for bread or wraps. This works out well since I try to avoid using processed ham and salamis.

Ingredients

large chicken (the larger, the better, depending on the size of your slow cooker)
½ pint of beer (based on a 5.6-litre slow cooker and as large a chicken as it can fit)
few sprigs of fresh rosemary
5 cloves of garlic
salt and pepper to season

Method

1. Half the garlic and rub it over the chicken.
2. Pierce the chicken all over with a sharp knife and insert the garlic pieces.
3. Pour the beer into the slow cooker pot.
4. Place the chicken in the slow cooker.
5. Generously cover with fresh rosemary.
6. Season with salt & pepper.
7. Cook on low for 8 hours (again, this is based on a large chicken to fill a 5.6-litre slow cooker).

TOP TIP

Place the chicken under the grill for a few minutes before serving, to give it a nice golden colour.

Popular family favourites that are easily adapted to your slow cooker

Lasagne

It might sound strange, but lasagne in your slow cooker is to die for! No need to adapt the recipe; simply place the raw lasagne noodles, sauce and toppings in the slow cooker and cook for 6 hours on low.

You might think that the result is mushy, overcooked pasta, but, on the contrary, the pasta is cooked to perfection and the ingredients blend so beautifully no one will ever believe it was slow cooked!

Soup

All soups can be made in the slow cooker.

Since the slow cooker tends to produce quite a bit of water from the slow cooking and condensation, reduce the water/liquid ingredient content to 25% of what the recipe calls for.

Once the soup is cooked, stir well, blend if required, taste, and if more water/liquid ingredient is required add them at the end.

Stews and curries

As with soup, cook as per recipe instructions but hold back on the water or liquid ingredient content. If the recipe calls for milk or cream, add it at the end, as the slow cooking might spoil it. If you are freezing, do not add the milk or cream to the whole batch, but only to the batch you are eating that day. When freezing extra portions, take note on the box of how much milk or cream should be added when heating up the food.

KEY POINTS

1. Meal planning holds the key to eating wholesome food which does not take too much time to prepare.

2. Once you plan ahead, you will be able to batch cook and allow yourself the grace of not cooking every day.

3. The freezer is a great tool for freezing foods you consume on a regular basis to be used in case of emergencies.

4. When selecting recipes, two of the following criteria must apply: the recipe must be quick to prepare, healthy, freezable, slow-cooked, or portable.

CHAPTER 4
PARENTING 101

"Children have never been very good at listening to their elders, but they have never failed to imitate them."
—James Baldwin

BUSY MAMAS MAKE FOR GREAT PARENTS

Being a stay-at-home mum doesn't automatically mean there is great parenting in the formula.

I am not in the least saying that stay-at-home mums are not good parents in the least. I am specifically refuting what the majority of working mums falsely choose to believe: that they are not good enough parents because they are not at home 24/7. Yes, I mean you!

Parenting tips for the busy mum

Being a good parent does not mean you need to be physically present at all times; however:

- **Make sure that you are always easy to reach** in case of minor emergencies. If you must go into a meeting and are unable to answer your phone, ask a trusted colleague to take your calls and advise you in case of an emergency.

- **Don't try to attend every single school event yourself.** It is virtually impossible to do so, that is unless you want to exhaust all of your leave days and stress yourself out. If your child is too little to understand, make sure that you or a close family member is present at events when the child is present. They will not understand why their friends all have a parent or relative present and they do not. If your kids are older, explain that you choose school events wisely in order to have enough days off left to care for them when they get sick and need you, and for quality time together. It goes without saying that major events should not be missed, such as the school play, parents' day, or meeting the teachers. Involve the children in the decision-making process. There might be a couple of events where someone else can attend in your place and a few others which are not so important and can be missed. Keep in contact with a few mums whose kids attend the same school as yours and get in touch to ask about a particular meeting, if need be.

- **Stay in touch with your child's carer, day in, day out.** You might not be there from 8 to 5, but little ways can help you to not lose sync with your child's routine. If your baby or little kid attends nursery or has a babysitter at home, keep a small notebook somewhere handy and ask your child's carer to fill out some basic notes about their day. These can include how much formula your baby is drinking, nap times, bowel movements, general behaviour, and a few of that day's activities.

- **Be upfront with your child's teacher.** He or she spends long hours daily with your child, thus it's very important that they are aware of anything significant in your child's life. If you are going through some hurdles or issues at home, such as separation, divorce, financial issues, be-havioural concerns, or anything else which is affecting your child's life, do make their teacher aware. Being aware of the situation will allow the educators to understand the child better and provide further support.

- **No one knows it all.** This is especially true when kids start getting older. The pre-teen and teen years are a scary age for parents, and your child can have meltdowns about matters that are actually pretty serious. We are lucky to have so much help in today's day and age. Do not feel scared or incompetent when reaching out to social workers, child psychologists, or parenting coaches. The valuable advice that they can offer can do a world of good.

- **Be honest with your child.** There is absolutely nothing wrong with your child knowing 'mummy's sad', or 'mummy has had a bad day', or 'mummy's grumpy'. On the contrary, such statements will help your child get in touch and learn how to deal with their emotions. Let them also watch you as you deal with your emotions. They will learn coping skills and develop their emotional intelligence.

- **Be consistent.** Giving in might be the easiest thing to do right now, but you are setting yourself up for long-term trouble. Today's children are wily beings, and they quickly learn that a tantrum, inconsolable crying, or whining your ear off can lead to them getting what they want.

EASIER WAYS TO ENCOURAGE GOOD BEHAVIOUR

Lead by example

The easiest and most foolproof way to do so is to be the best role model you can possibly be for your children. There is no better way to show your children how to behave, than by doing it yourself. Make it a point to be especially polite and courteous, kind and altruistic, and talk to your kids about it.

On a rainy day, assuming it's safe, stop your car in the road when you see someone trying to cross the road. Say, "Poor lady, it's raining and she would have got soaked had we not stopped to let her cross the road".

If someone at the supermarket drops change, help to pick up the coins. Say, *"I'm sure he would have lost some of his money had we not picked it up for him"*.

Let them know what's next

Children of all ages thrive on routine and predictability. Knowing what's next and what to expect gives children a sense of security and belonging and essentially fosters overall good behaviour.

Identify a timetable of sorts, as simple as it may be, and hang it on your child's noticeboard. For younger children, draw up a cardboard clock, colour-coded according to the different activities during the day.

For example, colour in as follows:

2 p.m. – 3 p.m. as quiet time
3 p.m. – 5 p.m. as playtime
5 p.m. – 6 p.m. as dinnertime
6 p.m. – 7 p.m. as bath & read time
8 p.m. as bedtime

You may use a clock for mornings, and another for evenings.

Younger kids

With smaller kids aged 2 or 3 to 7 or 8 (depending on the individual child), visual good behaviour prompts work well.

The classic reward chart comes in many forms but usually requires quite a bit of attention and upkeep.

A simpler version which is just as effective is the incentive jar. You may call it 'the pom-pom jar', 'pasta jar', 'pebble jar', or whatever tickles your fancy. The idea is that for every good deed or behaviour, one pom-pom, pasta shell, or pebble goes into the jar. When the jar is full, the child gets rewarded with a special treat or reward. The rewards needn't be big, and for the most part should be based on activities which promote quality time with the family, creativity, or recreation.

Ideas for rewards

Afternoon at the park

Ball game with mum

Board game

Movie night

Cake making activity

Extra bedtime story

Paper craft activity

Bike ride

'Make your own pizza' night

Treasure hunt

Water fight

Choice of dinner

Fun science experiment

Going out for ice cream

Extended bedtime (say 15-30 minutes at the weekend)

Cookie making afternoon

Stickers

Fun, educational outing

Pillow fight

Picnic with food of your choice

Sleepover with friends

Pick a dessert

Make a home-made smoothie

Indoor 'camping' for a night

Outdoor camping in the backyard (space and weather permitting)

1 make-up session on Mum

Drive-through lunch of your choice

Choose music to listen to in the car for a day

Whatever you do...

DON'T remove the pom-poms/pasta/pebbles from the jar. They have been placed there for good behaviour. Bad behaviour should not be tackled by dismissing any achievements.

DO lay out the rules beforehand. Be as clear as you can with your child about what's acceptable and what's not, and stick to your guns.

DON'T make the jar too big, or the pom-poms/pasta/pebbles too small. If you cannot find a balance, use a spoon and put in a 'spoonful' every time your child deserves a pat on the back.

DO react immediately. If a reward is due, do not let your child wait. Dole out deserved praise as soon as a target is reached and keep your promise by granting the prize within a matter of days. If it is not doable immediately, make a plan and inform your child accordingly.

Older kids - A tough nut to crack

You think you've got it under control until your child starts showing the first signs of adolescence, and then your world starts to crumble. Whatever techniques used to work are now useless, and your once 'controllable' child has morphed into a harder-headed, strongly opinionated, always right human being. I'm in no way insinuating that this period is similar to the toddler years or terrible twos—those couple of years are peanuts compared to this!

It sounds like older children take up more energy than smaller kids. In some cases, yes, they do. So how can we be more efficient in managing our teens with a sense of love and attention? It's so easy to throw your hands up in the air and give up.

A few pointers will help you feel better and put the right foot forward:

1. Remember, "It's just a phase"

The famous phrase that got us through our child's baby and toddler years is back! Hold on, this too shall pass.

2. Listen

Really and honestly listening to whatever your teen has to say shows you truly care. As petty as what they are saying might seem to you, remember, it matters to them.

EFFICIENCY TIP

Pair listening to your teen on a daily basis with another daily activity, such as a brisk walk around the block together or a commute with just the two of you. Not only will this help you to practise listening every day, but your child will know that if they need to talk you are always ready to hear them out at the same time every day.

---

3. Hold back on the nagging

As tempting as it may be, nagging has a negative effect and will not get anything done. Mum moans, teen rebels, no one wins. Next time you feel the need to nag, stop and think. Ask yourself if the request you are making is reasonable. If it is, be clear about your expectations. Set a time limit. Ask your child whether they have any issues with your demand. Inform them beforehand that you will remind them of that task. Explain the consequences if the required task is not handled appropriately. If they manage, praise them, but if they do not, impose the agreed upon consequences. They will learn.

Repeating this exercise every day can be draining. Take some time to go through your basic expectations with your child, such as homework, study work, hygiene, chores etc, and draw up a simple chart or 'agreement' which includes all of the above.

4. Don't react to their whining, complaints or comments with a quick solution or criticism

Replying with a simple *"Hmm"* and showing that you're listening will prompt them to open up and, more often than not, they will come to their own conclusions.

For example, it is very natural to respond to *"Mr Brown's test was so hard today!"* with, *"I told you you didn't study enough! I'm sure you would have done better had you put in a little more effort!"*. Do you think that this quip will help your child in any way? Imagine answering with *"Hmm"* or *"Boy does it sound like a tough test!"*. Your child will be more prone to following up with something like, *"It was the hardest test I've ever taken! I hope I don't fail! I guess I better revise a little more next time!"* A less positive reply from a prouder teen still reaps better results than the first reply.

5. Teach positively

This also relates to the previous point. We have ample time to teach our kids important life lessons. Remember that the right time is never in a reaction to an action. Find quiet moments when both of you are in good spirits to constructively criticise and educate your child in a calm and positive manner.

6. Choose your battles

Think before arguing. Ask yourself if it is worth fighting over. Fewer arguments equal less negative energy and fewer opportunities for conflict.

Common stumbling blocks and ways to help avoid them

Doling out punishments unwisely

You might be so angry at your child that you give out the first harsh punishment that comes to your head. Was it really such a good idea to tell your child there will be no picnic on Sunday when it is the only day of the week you were looking forward to, to spend time with your family?

Never react instantly to bad behaviour. It's perfectly OK to not know how to handle your child when they are rude out of the blue, or do something you did not expect. Be firm and let your child know that they have crossed the line and that you are angry or disappointed. Also let them know that you need to think about what they have done and talk about it later on in the day, when you are calm and have made a decision on the best way to handle it.

Handing out a punishment - but did your child learn anything?

Punishment is an old, scary word which I dislike strongly. In some instances, punishments are not appropriate at all.

Personally, I think that the appropriate form of punishment is consequences. Always think about the possible natural or logical consequence of the bad behaviour. For example, if your child doesn't want to sit properly in her chair during dinner, assume that it's unsafe for her to sit at the table and get her to eat standing or sitting on your lap like a 'little' child until she learns. If your child is giving you a hard time to leave the house on time, deduct the time she spent whining and wasting time from a favourite activity later on, because that time needs to be taken away from something or other. If she splashes water in the bath, she needs to clean it up…

It may sound cruel sometimes, but children need to learn that this is life, and that every action has a reaction.

Screaming and shouting to get things done

We've all succumbed to the pressure and raised our voice at some point or other, maybe even more so than we are willing to admit. The more you shout, the more immune your child will become to your raised voice, and before you know it your shouting is no longer effective.

EFFICIENCY TIP

What really works with younger kids is what I like to call 'the bucket of patience'. Giving your child a somewhat visual aid of your patience and showing them when you are at the end of your tether helps them to cut down on misbehaviour.

This is how it goes:

"You know, your mama has a bucket of patience, and right now it is full. Now what happens is, when you misbehave, the patience in the bucket starts getting less and less... Watch out because when my patience runs out and mama's bucket is empty, it means that mama is really, really angry."

Explain with your hands to show the size of the bucket and the level of patience as it starts to run out. I bet that your child's eyes will start to widen as soon as he or she realises that the bucket has almost been emptied!

Giving bedtime a negative vibe

If you send your child to bed when they misbehave, they will start to associate bedtime with punishment, and this gives bedtime a bad reputation. Bedtime is bound to start feeling like something negative if you are sent to bed every time you misbehave! Similarly, some parents give their children extra chores if they misbehave. I also disagree with this, since we do not want to teach our children that housework and chores are bad.

POSITIVE PARENTING

Positive parenting is not a difficult skill to master, and once you get the gist of it, it will save you precious time otherwise spent arguing with your child. An easy way to practise positive parenting is through your language. The way you present your words to your child makes all the difference in their reaction and their willingness to comply.

Say this, not that

Here are some helpful alternatives to commonly used phrases. Read aloud to yourself and put yourself in the shoes of your child to try to feel the difference between using one phrase and another.

What you might say	What to say instead
Don't shout!	Use your inside voice
You can't play with that!	Here, you can play with this
No hitting!	Use gentle hands
No running!	Walk, please
Don't touch anything!	Touch with your eyes
Don't eat with your hands!	Use your fork
Stop jumping up and down!	Come and sit down
Don't open the cupboard!	Please keep it closed
Don't throw things!	Take good care of that
Don't slam the door!	Close the door gently

PARENT-CHILD RELATIONSHIPS

Relationships were never created equal, and as complicated or unusual as your connection to your child might be, my 10 golden rules are a clear and basic mindset you can follow to build a strong foundation for your child's upbringing.

My 10 golden rules

1. Always present a united front. Mum and dad should never disagree in front of the child.

2. Plan some time every week to do something fun with your child, even if it's only for 20 minutes.

3. Don't use labels. Labels can be discouraging and limiting.

4. Apologise if needed. It will earn you respect.

5. Guide your children, but don't control them.

6. Show your child unconditional love. He or she will be more receptive.

7. Always keep your promises. Failing to do so will immediately render you untrustworthy. In case of unforeseen circumstances, sit down with your child and explain what has happened, and how you're going to fix it.

8. Never lie. Even if it's just a white lie. Find a way to simplify the matter at hand and give your child as little information as possible if you feel they are not ready for the full picture.

9. Be very clear about requests. Don't say: *"You didn't clean*

up after your snack". Instead, say *"I can see a dirty plate on the table, crumbs on the counter, and a napkin next to the sink. Please clear up"*.

10. Let them fail. This must be the hardest rule of all, but if you molly-coddle your child, they will never learn. Let them make mistakes and show them how to fix them. Be supportive, but let them lead.

KEY POINTS

1. Being a working mum doesn't make you less of a good mother.

2. Being a good mum does not mean you need to be physically present at all times. Being intentional with your actions will make a substantial and positive difference.

3. A foolproof way of encouraging our kids to behave appropriately is to be a good role model for them.

4. Parenting teens is a different story altogether to parenting toddlers or little kids and requires a great deal of patience and understanding.

5. Kids react completely differently and are more willing to comply when presented with a positive attitude and statements.

CHAPTER 5
HEALTH FIRST

"Let food be thy medicine and medicine be thy food."
—Hippocrates

THE BASICS

As the chapter title indicates, yes, health first! An under the weather parent really does throw everyone off balance, and sick kids only lead to stress and worry, which weaken our immune system and make us susceptible to even more sickness.

Easy ways to keep everyone's health in check

Sleep

The easiest way to promote well-being, and one of the most underrated and ignored. Getting enough good quality sleep is imperative for physical, mental, and emotional well-being, as well as for your safety and overall quality of life.

Eat well

Don't think about what you need to remove from your diet, but rather, think about what you need to add to make it more varied and healthier. This positive mind frame will encourage you to eat more wholesome foods and you will automatically start limiting healthy foods that are not as healthy once you start feeling so good.

Move

Being active improves your health dramatically and wards off serious diseases such as cancer, diabetes, and cardiovascular disease.

Be positive

Staying positive boosts your overall health. End the day with some gratitude and think about one thing to be grateful for every single day before you go to bed.

Laugh

Indeed, laughter is one of the best medicines! Laughing has so many incredible health benefits, such as lowering stress, boosting your immune system, improving cardiac health, and lowering blood pressure.

Leave your shoes outside

Just imagine bringing millions of the bacteria found outside into your home! This rings especially true if you have babies who are crawling.

Stand up straight

Besides giving one a more confident feel and look, having correct posture also carries other benefits. You already know that standing or sitting up straight is better for your back and your neck, but did you know that doing so will also enhance your mood? Great posture will reduce the stress hormone cortisol, and also help increase 'happiness' hormones serotonin and dopamine.

Wash your hands

I'm pretty sure you've got this one covered and fully understand the implications of not washing your hands before meals, or after using the bathroom, or as soon as you arrive

home, but do make sure your kids understand the consequences of not doing so too. Show them a few videos on
YouTube on why hand washing is important, and remind them
to do so when needed.

Stay hydrated

One is required to drink 3% of their body weight in order to get
enough fluids in. Drinking water combats fatigue, increases
energy, reduces headaches, flushes out toxins, and boosts
overall immunity, to name but a few benefits. I truly believe
and recommend that everyone in your family has a personal water bottle to ensure everyone is getting a fair amount.
Spice up plain water with cucumber and mint, lemon, or drink
sparkling water instead.

SOUND ADVICE

*Mobile phones, tablets, handbags, schoolbags,
and shopping bags are all items which carry
more bacteria than a toilet! Never, ever place
bags on tables or kitchen counters! Wipe down
your gadgets on a daily basis with disinfectant.*

Don't share your cup

I truly believe that drinking from the same glass contributes to
the spreading of germs and infections. Someone might not be
sick but might still carry bacteria, and someone might be sick
and might not be showing symptoms as yet.

Stick to your appointments

Be diligent with your own, and your family's medical appointments and schedule them as your GP or other medical advisors recommend. Make a reminder every year or two, depending on the frequency of the appointments, to call up and make an appointment, be it a blood test, dentist's appointment, eye exam, kids' yearly check-up and so on.

Your medicine stash

ORGANISATION TIP

Make a habit of having a well-stocked medicine cabinet to avoid having to go to the pharmacy every other day to buy something you have just ran out of, and to ward off sickness without delay.

Having said that, using a cabinet is certainly not the only method one may use to store medicine and, in fact, there are more practical ways of storing health-related products. The best way to store medicine that I have found is to put all our stock into various IKEA shoebox-sized boxes. This system is better than most conventional medicine storage methods because:

- You can use different boxes for different types of medicine, say cold & flu, stomach health, painkillers and fever, children's, etc.

- The size of the boxes is makes it easy to carry any one

out of the room to be able to look for something specific.

- Going through the boxes to check expiry dates is not a daunting task.

- Keeping everything neatly stored is easier than having all your medicine in one particular place.

- The chances of building up clutter are much less.

As soon as something runs out, add it to your 'pharmacy' list on your shopping app if you use one, or if you don't then make a note in your notebook so that you can conveniently buy whatever you need when you pop into the pharmacy.

Once in a while, go through your stock and check the expiry dates. Toss anything which is expired or has no use.

Buy first aid kits from your local pharmacy and always keep one in your home as well as in your car.

PRACTICAL HEALTH HACKS FOR MUMS

Simple but effective tips

1. Store aloe vera in the fridge and use it for sunburns and any other topical burns. The cooling effect is so much more relieving than using it straight out of the bottle.

2. If your kid gets a splinter, make a baking soda paste using a generous amount of baking soda and water. There's no rule to how much water you add, as long as the result is a paste-like consistency. Put the paste onto the splinter,

cover with a large plaster, and let the magic happen. After an hour, the splinter should be easily removable by scraping it off.

3. Sore throat? Soothe your child's throat with marshmallows. This may sound a bit too good to be true, but the research seems to add up. Apparently, the gelatin in the marshmallows contributes to soothing a sore throat. This is especially handy for kids who are too little to take lozenges for fear that they might choke on them, or kids who resist taking them at all. Be aware that marshmallows are still classified as a choking hazard. If you opt to go down this road, I would suggest that you cut up the marshmallows into little square-shaped pieces and monitor your child whilst they are eating them.

4. A spoonful of sugar helps the medicine go down! No, not really, but there are a few tips which can help! For older kids, ask them to hold their nose while they take their medicine; the taste is much less potent if they cannot smell the syrup. For younger kids, administering the medicine with a dropper down the side of the mouth is definitely helpful. At times, the taste can be masked by mixing the medicine with yoghurt or flavoured milk. Always speak to your doctor or pharmacist because some syrups can be substituted with suppositories. If not, there might be the option of an alternative medicine which is administered over a shorter period of time.

5. Stop a coughing fit. If your child is coughing in the middle of the night, try rubbing a menthol and eucalyptus rub on the soles of their feet instead of their back.

6. Administer suppositories the easy way. This works on babies and little kids. If and when possible, try administering suppositories to your baby whilst they are asleep. You will need to turn the child on their side and use plenty of petroleum jelly. I've tried this with my little one who went through a couple of bouts of fever as a baby, and it worked wonders. She wouldn't even notice!

7. If your kids are allergic to a medicine, keep a digital note on your smartphone. Send an email to yourself or save the information on the cloud (such as Google Drive and Notes). Chances are, if you are in a stressful situation, you will not remember the name of the medicine.

8. Keep an A5 folder for each kid with important medical information in it. Store things such as your child's baby book, any medical/hospital appointment papers, immunisation information, and any other paperwork. Stick a label on the front with the child's name, date of birth, ID number and blood type.

9. If your child is suffering from a condition, or you are facing health issues, as small or worrisome as they might be, take notes and put them away for safekeeping in this folder. You might be asked specific questions later on or might need to refer to them to see what medicine your child was taking, if anything was affecting their condition, and so on.

NOT JUST CONVENTIONAL MEDICINE

I am a firm believer in medicine; however, I am also of the opinion that whatever medicine can be avoided, should be avoided. Our body is designed to fight infections and disease, and if we can supplement ourselves to help our bodies do this naturally, kudos to us!

Whilst alternative medicine replaces conventional medicine completely, complementary medicine is designed to work in harmony with traditional medicine and therapies.

There are several doctors that are all for complementary options. If you too feel more comfortable having your family and yourself treated as such, 'shop around' until you find a doctor that prescribes such options.

Remedies you can try

Epsom salts

Epsom salts are so severely underrated! We use these in our home, and I can vouch that they are truly effective. They're not expensive to buy and are simply added to a warm bath. Add a handful and soak for 30 minutes. They are helpful in more ways than one, including the following:

1. Relaxation

2. Pain relief: Muscle, joint, tension headaches, cramps, bruises

3. Reduction of blood sugar levels

4. Improvement of circulation and overall arterial health

5. Detoxification: Use after swimming in a chlorinated pool, or weekly to detoxify

6. Anti-inflammatory: Excellent for itchy skin, eczema, asthma, and allergies

Saline nasal spray

When we blow our noses, we are ridding our bodies of harmful bacteria, viruses and pathogens. If our noses are dry, which is usually the case in the winter, these cannot be flushed away.

Using a saline spray can help. Train your kids to use it daily in winter, especially after school, or after being holed up somewhere with a group of kids.

Essential oils

The potency of essential oils is not to be taken lightly, and they are to be used with caution. Did you know that the first ever recorded prescription in the world was for an essential oil? Essential oils work on the root of the problem and do not just mask symptoms.

Essential oil use in children

1. Essential oils are used topically on pulse points or affected areas. In the case of children it is recommended to always mix (a few) drops with aqueous cream or any lotion.

2. Use a few drops in diffusers, on pillows, bath towels, or sprayed in your home. The aroma in itself is beneficial.

3. Essential oils may also be added to your child's bath. I'm sure you've heard that this is widely popular with adults, but when it comes to children, the essential oil should be diluted in a carrier oil such as coconut or sweet almond

oil, or whole milk.

4. Essential oils are not to be used for babies younger than six months. From six months to two years only diffusing (in an oil diffuser) is recommended. If you would like to play it safe, start using these oils from two years onwards and consult with your child's paediatrician. Exercise extra caution if the child is asthmatic or suffers from other respiratory conditions as essential oils can aggravate the situation rather than ease it.

5. Do your research. Make sure that the oil you will be using on your child is safe to use for children.

6. Allergic reactions are no fun. Introduce one oil at a time. If your child is allergic to an oil, you can tell after 15 to 30 minutes after use. Please contact your child's doctor in the event of an allergy, just as you would do with any other allergic reaction.

More good stuff

Elderberry syrup

Elderberry syrup has been used for years and years to help boost immunity and combat colds and the flu. It is very effective in treating upper respiratory tract infections. The syrup can be taken by children and adults alike, both as prevention and treatment. My son who typically suffers from allergies and croup takes this all year round, and we find it to be extremely effective.

Quercetin

Quercetin is a natural anti-histamine and an ideal supplement for your kids (or yourself!) to take if they suffer from seasonal allergies and hay fever. Best to be used long-term for optimum performance.

Multivitamins

If your children are picky eaters it is better to resort to multivitamins rather than risk your children being nutritionally deficient. Buy a children's multivitamin that contains all the essential vitamins and some minerals and make sure this is taken on a daily basis. Check out the fine print, as quite a bit of multivitamins have an alarming amount of artificial sweeteners to help mask the vitamins' taste. Do not buy anything which has more than two grams of sweetener per dose, and avoid anything with artificial colouring.

Honey

Several studies show that honey is more effective than cough medicine for cough relief and actually helps children to have a better night's sleep.

Kids are happy to take it because it tastes so good. Give half a teaspoon to kids aged 1 to 5 and one teaspoon to kids aged 6 to 11 daily when they have a cough.

If you can get your hands on Manuka honey, all the better. Manuka honey is derived from the bee that feeds on the Manuka plant, found in New Zealand. Manuka honey is significantly more antibacterial and anti-inflammatory than traditional honey and comes with a UMF rating which indicates the MGO (enzyme) content of that particular Manuka honey. To put it simply, MGO is to Manuka honey what SPF is to sunblock.

Do not give honey to children younger than one year, because the bacteria found in it can cause a fatal condition called botulism.

Just for the parents (& older kids)

Oral antiseptic solution

This is my go-to magic solution for when I start feeling the dreaded symptoms of a cold or flu: tickling in my throat, a slight earache, and difficulty swallowing.

Simply gargle three times a day for three to five days *as soon* as you feel a symptom, as slight as it might be. It's so good to be true you might think that the only thing you are doing is delaying the inevitable, but oral antiseptic solutions are excellent for killing viruses, bacteria, and fungus infections alike.

STAYING HEALTHY

Stop spreading germs!

If someone in the family is sick, a little extra caution will go a long way. Being very careful will help to stop spreading the sickness. The same applies to your place of work, which is a little tougher, since you do not have much control over your surroundings and those around you, but still possible with a little thought.

Step 1: Disinfect

If a family member is sick, make a habit of regularly wiping down doorknobs and light switches with *tissue paper* and disinfectant. Using tissue paper is key here since you do not want to use a reusable cloth as this would only smear the bacteria all over the place, instead of eliminating it.

Three times a day, using one paper for each knob/light switch, do a quick wipe down. Also wipe down surfaces, remotes, phones, laptops, and the like.

At work, disinfect your desk area or office; however, once you visit the bathroom and wash your hands always open the doors back to your office with tissue paper. You might think I'm slightly mad, but if you were to stop and think how many people sneeze in their hands without washing them, or actually use the toilet and do not wash their hands, you would be shocked!

Step 2: Wash your hands more often

Enough said.

Step 3: Avoid touching your face

More specifically, avoid touching your nose and mouth, as germs can enter your body through them.

Step 4: Stay away

Try not to get too close. It's more difficult if your children are sick, of course, but take all other necessary precautions and at the very least do not let your face get too close to theirs. Ask them to stay in their rooms as much as possible. If you have more than one bathroom, it would be ideal that the sick person uses one bathroom and the other is used by the rest of the family members. Do not let sick family members cook or be in close proximity of food. If a sick workmate offers tea, decline politely!

Step 5: No sharing

Never, ever, use a sick person's pillow, sheets, or toys, or in the case of work, a mouse, calculator, or otherwise. Ditch the hand towels and the tea towel, and use disposable napkins.

Step 6: Teach your children good habits

Show your children the correct way to sneeze. If a tissue is readily available, they should sneeze into a tissue and throw it away promptly, and, if not, teach them how to sneeze into their elbows instead of their hands. In the case of your workmates, well, lead by example...they *just* might take the hint!

Step 7: Toss the tissues

Keep a small plastic bag within reach and always throw away tissues immediately after use. Keep the bag closed; make a light knot so it may be reopened.

Step 8: Let the sunshine in

Open the windows to let the air circulate a few times a day. If possible, go out for a brisk walk and get some air yourself.

Get your groove on

Running, tennis, the gym, or any other type of exercise that gets your blood pumping, is good for you! I envy people who make exercise a priority and truly enjoy getting hot and sweaty whilst giving their body a terrific workout.

You might be into all this but your current lifestyle does not allow you the time to be as dedicated as you once were.

Stop feeling like a failure and commit to moving as opposed to exercising. Fitness needn't mean sticking to a rigorous work-out routine, come rain or shine.

SOUND ADVICE

Making movement a natural part of your everyday life is the true meaning of fitness and ultimately health.

Try to incorporate at least five of the following into your day:

1. Park your car a block away from your destination and walk. If you're using public transport get off one stop away.

2. Walk instead of drive wherever possible.

3. Take the stairs instead of the lift.

4. Do some jumping jacks or stretching exercises whilst you are waiting for the kettle to boil.

5. Do some squats at your desk whilst replying to emails.

6. Take your children to the playground and run around after them. Play with them, instead of watching them.

7. Choose to go for long weekend walks with your family.

8. Walk around when you're on the phone. Pop a pair of wireless headphones into your ears and move around instead of sitting still.

9. Do more in person. Instead of sending out an email, or making a phone call to your workmate, go to see him or her in person.

10. Dance. Pump up the music when you're at home and dance! You can prance about happily whilst you are clearing up; get your kids to join in your happy dance!

11. Play with your kids when you're home. If you have a yard, go out and kick a ball. Give them piggyback or pony rides on your back. Play hide and seek, or catch. Have fun!

12. Move on the hour. Set an alarm to remind yourself if need be! Every hour, get up from your desk or stop whatever you're doing and stretch. Jog on the spot for two minutes.

Superfoods

I'm sure you already do your best to eat healthy, whole foods most of the time. Some of us are blessed with being so health conscious that they don't bat an eyelash when surrounded by sweet temptations or irresistible, naughty foods. I am a firm believer in balance and eating what feels right for your body.

SOUND ADVICE

Focus on adding rich, nutrient dense foods to your diet, rather than eliminating foods and restricting yourself.

This list of superfoods is vast; here are the ten which I feel are the most appealing to adults and kids alike.

1. Oats

Packed with fibre and zinc, oats help lower cholesterol, aid in fighting off infection and boost overall immunity. Go to Chapter 3 for my favourite oat recipe: 'Overnight Oats in a Jar'.

2. Eggs

Eggs were previously given a bad reputation, but now they have been given the all clear. Eggs are one of the *most* nutritious foods on the planet.

3. Sweet potato

This sweet vegetable is highly nutritious. It's packed with Vitamin A, along with a long list of other vitamins and nutrients. Kids love it because it tastes delicious! Serve mashed, or baked as 'sweet potato fries'. Yum!

4. Yoghurt

Buy plain Greek yoghurt and dress it up with honey, fresh fruit, dark chocolate, coconut, or granola! We also use it instead of cream or mayo in our home. Yoghurt is brilliant for your gut health, and the number of good bacteria you can get from eating this simple food item is immense. Steer clear of the sugary versions!

5. Lentils

Lentils can be very easily added to stews and soups and can be blended too. They are the best source of plant protein and contain a good amount of fibre too.

6. Avocado

It is recommended that 25% to 35% of calories in kids' diets should come from good fats. This is where the avocado comes in! Make guacamole, use avocado as a spread, mash it with a boiled egg and add a dollop of Greek yoghurt, or add it to salads.

7. Salmon

Containing all of the Omega-3 fatty acids, salmon is another great source of good fats. Try to buy wild salmon as opposed to farmed since the former is lower in mercury and higher in nutrients. Serve grilled with lemon and avocado on the side, or make some mouth-watering salmon fish cakes.

8. Apples

They say, "An apple a day keeps the doctor away", and with good reason. Packed with fibre and vitamins C, K, and some vitamin B and potassium, they are great for heart health, reducing the risk of diabetes, Alzheimer's, and cancer, amongst other benefits. Apples make a great snack due to their portability, and there are so many delicious treats one can make with them!

9. Spinach

Dubbed as one of the world's healthiest foods, spinach is nutritiously packed with vitamin K and C, potassium and fibre, helps control blood sugar, improves bone density, reduces blood pressure, and lowers the risk of asthma and cancer. Spinach is amazingly versatile and can be added to soups, omelettes or frittatas, smoothies, pasta, or patties. Pre-packed baby spinach can be easily incorporated as a side dish to a lot of main meals.

10. Wholegrain bread

Was there ever a kid who didn't love carbs? Opt for wholegrain as this is chock-full of fibre and tastes great!

KEY POINTS

1. Before everything else, take measures to keep your family's health in check.

2. A few health hacks will help you deal with common ailments such as splinters, sunburn, night cough, and more, as well as get organised in the health department.

3. Take extra caution when a family member is sick to stop spreading the sickness. The same applies to your place of work.

4. Do not fret if you cannot commit to a regular exercise routine. Staying active as part of your daily routine is just as beneficial and easier to manage.

5. Including superfoods and non-conventional medicine in your diet and lifestyle can help you stay on track and ultimately help you avoid getting sick!

CHAPTER 6
IT'S ALL ABOUT THE MONEY, HONEY

"Money does not dictate your lifestyle. It's what you do to get it and how you manage your finances that determine your lifestyle."
—Wayne Chirisa

SIMPLIFYING FINANCE

Here are four steps to easy budgeting without having to break out the calculator and wad of paper (or a spreadsheet), as well as handy tips to help you save and increase your income. These will make the financial part of your life less terrifying, no matter how much you earn and how much money you have. All you need to do is to make a plan once a year and stick with it.

The basics

The number one rule is to have a 'rainy day fund'. Save up enough money to get you through three to six months of un-employment if you are unfortunate enough to face this, or to have enough cash to resort to in the case of an emergency.

Once you have this emergency fund set up, move on to my 4-step rule.

The 4-step rule

Split your wage into four:

1. Bills account
2. Long-term savings
3. Short-term savings
4. Spending account (Split this into home & personal)

Step 1: Bills account

Some super-simple maths is needed here and it only a one-time requirement. List all of the bills and expenses you pay on a yearly basis: water, electricity, gas, fuel, phone bills, internet, medical, TV, loan or mortgage, car services, insurances. Add these up and then divide this total by 12. This is the amount you need to set aside each month for your bills.

Step 2: Long-term savings

Saving is already no fun at all, and it's even more dismal if you do not think about what you are saving for. Putting aside money month after month and watching the figure grow slowly, with no intention or plan, is about as exciting as watching paint dry. Have a goal. Think about what you want to do long-term. It might be that you are saving up for a down payment on a new house, putting aside money to invest in a business or stocks, or saving up for your children's education. Whatever it is, have a plan. Decide on a monthly figure to go towards this.

Step 3: Short-term savings

Short-term savings help you set achievable goals and deter you from spending money on meaningless things; in the end, everything adds up, even the small spends. You could be saving up for something as simple as a family photo shoot, or a new coat you've been eyeing, or a fun but costly day out to a fun-park with the children. Whatever it is, make it attainable, and put some money towards short-term savings every month.

Step 4: Spending account

After you decide on how much should be set aside for steps one to three, the rest is your spending power. Divide this into categories A and B:

(A) Set aside an amount to be spent on groceries.
(B) The rest is to be used to meet your own and your family's requirements, as you see fit.

SPLITTING YOUR WAGE

Your options

- **The good old envelope system**. Withdraw the cash, particularly the cash for Step 3 and Step 4, and place in separate envelopes. Your bills are easier paid online; so no need to withdraw here.

- **Online accounts.** Create separate accounts for separate purposes.

- **Using an app.** There are several apps which do all of the groundwork for you. I would not suggest opting for an app which will help you budget on a micro-management scale. Instead, opt for an app to which you can dictate your income, your savings amount, your bills, and in turn the app will let you know your daily spending amount. All you need to do is log in what you spend and the app will do the rest for you. Daily Budget is such an app—personally tried and tested and comes free of charge.

HOW TO HAVE MORE MONEY

Money-related hacks

- Use the luxury of online internet banking services and skip the queues at the bank. It's as safe, if not safer, more accessible, and is available 24/7.

- Set up automatic payments for your bills wherever possible. Besides avoiding late payment charges altogether, you can also save. Some companies offer a small discount in return for automatic, recurring payments.

- Scan or take a photo of all your paper bills and save them online on the cloud such as iCloud or Google Drive. Less clutter, more convenience.

Little ways to generate extra income

- Sell your old gadgets on eBay, even if broken. You would be flabbergasted if you knew how much cash your old mobile phone with the broken screen could earn you. Gadgets, as broken as they might be, are made up of tiny little pieces costing big money which are valuable to anyone looking for parts to fix the same model.

- Sell anything for the matter! eBay is easy to use; just make sure that you take note of the commission fees eBay (and Paypal) charge before setting your prices.

- Pack up all of your unused items and take the lot to a car boot sale.

- Become a pet sitter. This is especially valid if you already have your own pets and own a house with an outdoor area.

- Have a side hustle. A side hustle is a way to generate extra income *alongside* your already existing job. Be clever and see if you can make this work with something you are already doing as a hobby.

Little ways to save money

- Use the 20-day rule. If you set your eyes on something costly, wait 20 days and sleep on it before taking a decision. The 20 days will most definitely deter you from spending if your prospective purchase was guided by passion.

- Ditch the little but expensive habits. A modest purchase can go a long way. Something as simple as not buying that daily coffee-to-go can save you hundreds over the course of one year!

- Keep a gift stash. When the sales are on, keep your eyes open for gifts suitable for anyone in the family, and a couple of kids' gifts on hand for last minute party invitations.

- Buy clothes during the sales. This is especially important to do when your children are little since they grow out of their clothes so quickly! Shop around during the sales, and buy items you like with great prices in larger sizes for the next year or two.

- Shop the cheaper supermarket for your basics and regular needs.

- Never go to the supermarket hungry.

- Make homemade lunches for you and the family, and pack snacks to take with you when you are out and about for the day.

- Use cash instead of a credit card. This weighs a little heavier on you psychologically, so you end up spending less.

KEY POINTS

1. Budgeting needn't be a scary prospect. Breaking it down will simplify the process no matter how much money you have or earn.

2. Before everything else, set up an emergency fund to get you through 3-6 months of unemployment.

3. There are only four steps to budgeting. It is as easy as A-B-C.

4. Once you follow my 4-step rule, divide your cash accordingly and stick to your plan.

5. A few well-thought-out lifestyle changes can save you hundreds of euros each year!

It's all about the money, honey

CHAPTER 7
ON THE JOB

"Have regular hours for work and play; make each day both useful and pleasant, and prove that you understand the worth of time by employing it well. Then youth will bring few regrets, and life will become a beautiful success."
—Louisa May Alcott
(Little Women)

MORNINGS

The most effective way to get everyone out of the house, fed, dressed, and on time is to prepare all the things you will need in the morning the night before. This gives you more time to plan and leaves less room for error and forgetfulness.

Everyone's outfit should be prepared the night before. I lost count of how many times we ran out of clean socks the night before school, or couldn't find something or the other, or realised my husband had no ironed shirts left!

Kids & school

Teach your kids to do as much as they can in the morning. Kids aged seven and older can get dressed on their own; just make sure that their school uniform is within reach.

Schoolbags should always be checked the night before, and any paperwork filled out and ready to go. Prepare lunches which may be refrigerated overnight and packed into schoolbags in the morning.

Create a calming bedtime routine for each child depending on their age. Little kids usually thrive on the 'wash teeth, read a book' routine, whilst it is a good idea to get older kids to lower the light and read for half an hour every day before lights out. Many mamas struggle with getting their kids to read, and scheduling the last half hour before bedtime each evening ensures that this essential part of their daily routine is not overlooked.

Get your kids to bed on time. Kids need more sleep than you think to support their mental and physical development. Toddlers and pre-schoolers need around 11-14 hours of sleep per night, school kids aged 6 to 13 need 9-11 hours, and teenagers need 8-10 hours. Well-rested kids make for more reasonable beings!

Quick tips for the morning

1. If you are driving your kids to childcare or school, aim to arrive at work 30 minutes earlier. If one of your kids has a tantrum, spills milk, or finds it hard to wake up, you will still be punctual. If you get to your place of work earlier and are under extra pressure, deal with any pressing work issues that require that extra ounce of peace and concentration. If you can afford to get a bill paid online or reply to a personal email, use your time wisely and get some tasks out of the way.

2. If you own one bathroom and are a family of three, schedule bathroom times for each family member.

3. Create a morning to-do list for each kid: wake up, wash your face, get dressed, have breakfast, wash your teeth, put on your jacket & shoes, pick up your schoolbag, and GO! This can be affixed to a notice board in their bedroom.

4. Make breakfast as easy as possible. Cereal and fruit are convenient options. Lay all the dry foods on the table the night before and teach the little kids how to make their own cereal. Refer to Chapter 3 for some easy and nutritious recipes, some of which work well as takeaway breakfasts

to eat in the car for extremely busy mornings.

5. If there's anything you need to remember or anything you need your partner to get done in the morning, jot it down on a piece of paper and leave the paper in a pre-agreed place. Leave small reminders such as: 'slow cooker, 8 hours, low' or 'pack fruit salad'.

6. Wear your housecoat or bathrobe over your work outfit up until the last minute. Your outfit will remain intact in case of any morning messes, be it spilt milk, baby spit up, or orange juice.

Commuting to and from work

Now that you're a mum, you have probably discovered the joys of commuting, where you get to sit down for an uninterrupted half-hour.

In the morning, take your time to enjoy the blissful peace. Even if you usually drive your kids to nursery or school in the morning, they are usually still half asleep in the wee hours of the morning and will have no problem in sharing your desire.

Being able to just be contentedly silent will get you set for a really productive day.

If you're driving, you can also use your hands-free kit to get a couple of things done. Most likely the afternoon or evening drive is better suited to the following:

*   Make appointments and ask the person on the other end to confirm via email/SMS so that this would serve as your reminder.

- Call back that customer care agent about your phone/internet/TV issue and sit back whilst they take their time to transfer you from one person to the next

- Call your girlfriends for a quick catch or to set a girls' night out

- Return any calls you had no time to respond to

If you're not in the mood for chatting, put on some music and relax, sing along with the kids or, if you're alone, listen to your favourite podcasts.

Checklist: Essentials to keep in your car

A few essentials in the car will save you from having to pack up and leave when all goes awry!

The basics

- Plastic bags (to throw away random pieces of food or keep soiled clothes in)

- Disposable raincoats

- First aid kit

- Large bottle of water (for accidents or refilling your wiper water if it runs out)

- Small change for supermarket trolleys

- Some money for emergencies

- Pen and small notebook

- Basic, comfortable, flat shoes

- Packet of wipes
- Tissues
- Umbrella

For babies and younger kids

- Spare complete outfit
- Emergency nappies
- Spare snack
- Spare dummy, and/or any other comforter
- Travel potty

WORK & HOME

Finding balance

An imbalance between work and family is one of the most common sources of stress and anxiety. In today's fast-paced world, many women struggle to find a work-life balance.

More often than not, priority is given to one area, often resulting in a sense of guilt and failure. This often causes tension at home which may lead to heated arguments and a dysfunctional familial environment, both of which are extremely unhealthy for children and adults alike.

> ## SOUND ADVICE
>
> *Once you become a parent, it is so important to set boundaries, and not only for yourself, but also for your boss and colleagues.*

Here are a few simple tips to follow in this regard:

1. Be very clear with the people around you about your hours and do not apologise for not being there at all times.

2. Park your guilt! You only have yourself to answer to.

3. If it makes you feel better, set up an 'out of office reply' for the hours when the office is running and you are not in, with a clear reference to what to do and who to contact if immediate assistance is required.

4. Learn how to respond to impossible requests such as a 5 p.m. meeting when you definitely cannot make it since the childcare centre is closed at that time. Do not use the words "I cannot", but say "I don't" instead. "I don't work after 4:30 p.m." sounds much better than "I cannot".

Adjusting your work schedule to fit your new lifestyle

You may ponder the idea of switching to part-time hours, but a number of careers and positions do not permit this. However, working full-time needn't necessarily mean a conventional 9 to 5 job. Read on for some ideas on how to make your life easier in the work department. If you're a valuable asset to your company, you'd be surprised how accommodating they will be!

- Ask for reduced hours (say a 6-7 hour day) or a 4-day week.

- If you work in an office, consider working one day a week from home. Whilst your normal day of work will still need to be done at home, you can do the laundry whilst you work. Cutting out commuting time means that you save more time and can easily fit in a load or two of washing, drying, and folding (subject to having a tumble dryer of course).

- Flexitime is another option. Get to work earlier and leave earlier. If you're two adults in the house, a great way to make this work is for one of you to take the early shift, and the other the late shift. For example, in my case, I start the day earlier and take my youngest to nursery in the morning, then my husband takes over the evening shift and deals with bath time and bedtime whilst I squeeze in clearing up after dinner and clearing the house, cooking, and at the end of it all, getting some me time. Leaving before rush hour each morning and afternoon saves not just time, but stress.

- Ask if it's possible to give up your break to leave earlier.

- Use your break wisely, a myriad of things can be done during the time you usually spend eating and on the phone: shopping for groceries online, making menu plans, making grocery lists, paying bills online, budgeting, creating task lists, going for a quick errand—the list is endless.

Of course, there are plenty of jobs which allow for reduced, part-time, or work from home options. You might feel that it is better to cut down on hours to be able to spend more time at home.

SOUND ADVICE

Finding a work-life balance doesn't mean that you need to allocate equal time to each. Trust your instincts and do what feels right and what works for your family, lifestyle, and situation.

Running your own business

If you run your own business, finding a balance will prove to be more challenging. Despite being your own boss and being able to manage your own time, the odds of successfully finding a balance are significantly low.

Just as you would schedule time for work if you need to go to an office or store, you will need to schedule time to get your work done from home.

As your children grow, you can start to explain to them that you work from home for them to be able to find you there when they get home from school, and as they wake up each morning. Let them know that at some points during the day, and this especially applies to weekends and school holidays, even though you are home you need time to concentrate and to work.

Working from home does not mean you need to do it all. Have family pitch in, consider nursery school, summer school, sports clubs or play dates.

YOUR TIME AT WORK

Being a working mum means that most often than not we do not have the luxury of working late at short notice, which in turn means we have to be extra sharp with managing our time and meeting deadlines. Working mums are often considered as multi-tasking pros, which we are! Our home/kids workload equals more than two full time jobs which, in comparison, makes our job seem a breeze!

Making the most of it

A few simple hacks and tricks can help you perform better. The following is definitely not rocket science; you probably know it all, but bringing it all together will show you how easy it is to be more productive.

Let's start with the absolute basics: your workspace.

1. Keep your desk area clean, tidy, and clutter free. Have a look around your office. Is there anything you haven't used in a while? Donate anything still in working condition, and toss anything which is not working and irreparable. If you do not work in an office, and still have an assigned space, still try to keep it as organised as you can manage.

2. Organise the drawers closest to your desk in a way that

everything is easy to find. Make sure the contents are items you use on a regular basis.

3. If you have any other drawers or filing cabinets in your office which are not in such close proximity, use these to store papers and items which are equally as important but not used on a day-to-day basis.

4. Use paper trays to facilitate sorting of papers going in and out of your office and pending items.

5. Do you really need all that paper? In today's day and age, most papers can be scanned and stored safely on your network. Another bonus: if stored diligently, it's also easier to find, and for other people to follow up on if an emergency crops up!

6. Work comfortably. Your monitor and keyboard should sit right in front of you at eye level. If you're up on your feet all day make sure you are wearing comfortable shoes.

7. Whilst family photos and mementos are a nice addition to any workspace, watch out that they don't distract you. If they do, it's time for them to go.

8. Use a headset instead of a telephone. Work more efficiently by using both hands to type or do manual work whilst you are on the phone.

EFFICIENCY TIP

Get yourself a desk plant. Having a plant or flowers at your desk will help you focus better and increases productivity. Strange, but true!

9. If you share an office with other people, wear headphones when you need to concentrate and when you very politely need to ask others not to disturb you for no apparent reason.

10. Keep two smart notebooks: one for meetings, and another for your daily to-do list. Carry both with you, and use your personal one during any valuable waiting time to help you catch up.

11. Personally, I prefer a digital online to-do list: clutter free and accessible from anywhere. I like to categorise mine and have different colours for different subjects and colleagues. If I happen to chance upon a moment when both my co-worker and I are free to talk, I can quickly go over what's pending with him/her by glancing at my monitor.

Good daily habits

Just as you have a good daily routine at home, the same is needed at your workplace. Dozens of tasks will throw you off-balance if an established regime is not instilled. Fortunately, an easy daily schedule and a few good habits can ensure that what needs to be done, is done.

Start your day by checking your calendar. Make sure you are prepared for any meetings taking place that day.

Check your email. Get rid of any junk, reply to any emails which need a quick reply, and leave the rest in your inbox.

Next, review your to-do list. Get reoriented with it and cross off anything which has been accomplished.

Follow up. Go through your 'sent items' email folder. Check any emails which need following up to.

Once you have reviewed your calendar, email (in and out) and your to-do list, it should be perfectly clear which task to manage first.

Drink lots of water. Get yourself a refillable water bottle to keep yourself hydrated. Drinking a good amount of water will also motivate you to get up and move for bathroom breaks.

Take short but regular breaks. Get up from your chair at least once every hour, if not to refill your water or to go to the bathroom, then say hello to your colleagues, get two minutes of fresh air, or just walk around and take a breather.

Lack of inspiration? Get up, and get out for a minute or two. You're guaranteed to come back in a better state of mind.

Reassess your to-do list a couple of times throughout the day.

Prioritise intelligently.

Learn to say no. This smart move will enable you to allocate the required time to what you say yes to.

Learn how to delegate. You cannot do it all.

Take note of any daunting tasks and tackle them first thing in the morning, when energy levels run higher, and your mind is fresher.

One hour before the end of your workday, have another look at your to-do list and 'sent items' emails, just to make sure you have not left out anything significant.

Before closing your day, try to take the time to rewrite your to-do list on a fresh notebook page, and highlight anything which should be given high priority. If you are working with a digital list, have a final look at it and review accordingly.

Take a moment to reflect and plan your next day's work. Add notes to your to-do list or schedule any important tasks in your calendar with set reminders.

WHEN THE GOING GETS TOUGH

All's well when everything is hunky-dory and your routine is followed day in, day out without any major interruptions. That's until one dreaded morning, in an all too familiar hoarse voice, your child says to you, *"Mum, I feel sick"*.

Sudden illnesses

A child's sudden illness can throw working mums into panic mode. How do you explain to your boss that you cannot make it to work that morning? How do you finish that big proposal that is due tomorrow?

Balancing work and motherhood already presents a huge emotional and logistical challenge; put sick kids in the picture and this adds up immeasurably. The crux of it all is that sickness springs up on you like a snare and there is no right or wrong timing for it.

In the first year of childcare, nursery school, or big school, be prepared for having more sick days than you can count on both hands. Your child is being newly exposed to several types of bacteria and viruses and needs to (very unfortunately) weather a couple of them before his or her immune system catches on and starts fighting bugs off like there's no tomorrow. Don't despair, this period is usually short-lived. What looks like forever usually lasts one winter or two at the most.

How to be better prepared

- Planning for the worst means that nasty surprises don't have as tough an effect on you as if you had no backup plan at the ready. If you have family who live reasonably close and do not have a day job or work part-time discuss the option of having them as backup when your kids are sick.

- Keep a spare car seat or booster seat in the car of the person who is assigned as your backup. If someone else is available to pick up the kids in case of them being sick at school, or any other hiccup for that matter, it will save you having to leave your job if it could be helped. Ideally, there should be a car seat in every car in the household, so it does not have to be you who leaves the workplace to save the day every time.

- Provide your children's schools with copies of identity cards of all the people allowed to pick up your child from school. Make sure that the people who are allowed to do so carry their ID card with them when picking up your child.

- Of course, there's sick and there's *sick.* Our job, first and foremost, is being mothers, and our careers have to take the backseat if the need arises. Discuss this with your boss. There's no shame in it. Explain that your child will, in all probability, need you a little bit more in the first year or so of school, and that you are ready to make up for it as long as he trusts that you will prioritise responsibly and intelligently. Let him or her know of your backup plan that is in place and that, ultimately, if all else fails, or if your child is very sick and needs his or her mom, you will need to stay home. Working from home in one-off scenarios might be an option.

- If you're married or have a partner, take staying at home with sick kids in turns. When one of us needs to stay at home with our sick kids, my husband and I both look at our calendars and deadlines and decide who has to stay home according to our workload and meetings for the day. Sometimes we split the day. I stay home for the first couple of hours and then we switch.

- If you run your own business the same decisions need to be taken. You might not have a boss to answer to, but you still have deadlines to respect and clients to keep happy. Do not take everything for granted because you can be more flexible. Respect your business and act as though you have a boss to answer to.

- There are specific babysitting companies that are very good at providing sitters to care for your sick one provided that you inform them what the child is suffering from and give ample instructions on medicine dosages.

See to it that your child's immunity is well taken care of by feeding them plenty of greens and fruit and avoiding processed foods as much as possible.

KEY POINTS

1. The secret to drama-free mornings is to prepare as much as you possibly can in the evenings.

2. Maximise your limited time at home in the morning by implementing a few rules and following a few tips.

3. Finding a good balance between work and home is crucial to your sanity.

4. Get organised at work and implement good daily habits. Working mums really need to give their 200% 100% of the time since, more often than not, they cannot afford to work late at short notice.

5. Make a plan on how to handle a sick child and do not wait for your child to get sick to work this out.

CHAPTER 8
HAPPY MAMA, HAPPY FAMILY

"Take time off...
The world will not fall apart without you."
—Malebo Sephodi

LETTING GO OF THE GUILT

I am sure that most of you working mums reading this book have experienced a tremendous amount of guilt. You might have felt it when you just returned to work after maternity or parental leave, or even years down the line. These feelings may come and go and are especially present when we face situations over which we have no control, hence we feel the need to at least blame someone, and we often end up blaming ourselves.

One of the intentions of this book is to help you ease some of the guilty feelings that weigh you down so often.

Quick tips - How to deal with guilt

1. Ask yourself: Have you done something wrong? Think about why you're feeling guilty. Did you make a bad choice? Accept that it's OK for work to come before your kids sometimes. It all depends on the nature of the situation.

2. Take time off when you can. Remember to take care of yourself! Stop and recharge your batteries. Take a day off and treat yourself to a spa day or a lazy day, or even a few hours if you can't afford a full day. Take time to remember that besides a mum, and a career lady, you're YOU!

3. Lower the bar. Accept that there is no 'perfect' when it comes to parenting. Being a mother is hard enough without the ridiculously high standards and 'perfect' ways we should parent our children. There's no need to be a perfect

mum to be a good mum! Remember: present over perfect!

4. Distance yourself from people who cause you guilt. Did someone just say something to make you feel guilty? If you can, get some space from them. If not, try to learn to block their silly little arguments.

5. Keep in mind that we all have our challenges. Rest assured, stay-at-home mums have guilty feelings too. We yearn so hard to be the best, that we often put the blame on ourselves for no apparent reason. Give yourself a break!

6. Don't dwell on the time spent away from your children. Remind yourself of all the benefits you and your family get out of you being a working mum. There is no such thing as a perfect work-life balance, but by reading this book you are trying your best—and that is good enough!

TAKING CARE OF YOURSELF

Taking care of yourself plays such an important part towards your health and happiness.

A confident, productive, happy, and healthy mother is able to raise very happy kids, can excel at work, and is able to manage day-to-day tasks successfully (at least most of the time—and when not, does not feel like a failure!).

Just like you are advised not to give up your identity once you are married, the same goes for when you have children. It is true that you have less time to yourself, but be sure to *make* time for yourself.

Why you should make time for yourself

- Nothing teaches your kids self-respect like seeing you make time for yourself. Show them YOU matter. You are not just the person who cooks, cleans, and takes care of them. You are a brilliant, interesting, passionate woman who is creative, takes care of herself and her needs, and balances her life intelligently. Your children will learn from you by example!

- When you take time for yourself, you relax and stress levels decrease. You smile more, are calmer, and have an overall better outlook of the world. All these things will make you a better parent, and an overall better person, be it at home or work.

- Being a parent is hard. Granted it is very rewarding; however, self-care is a priority if you are to be a great mum, career woman, and wife (aka Supermum).

- Absence makes the heart grow fonder. Going AWOL for a brisk 30-minute walk gives your children time to appreciate you.

- Your children will not be young forever. What will happen when they move out and live independently? Would you still know who you really are?

How to make more time for yourself

Here are another handful of tips and tricks to give you *even more* time for yourself.

1. Stay off those apps. You might be an app junkie and spend countless minutes 'quickly checking' your social media feed. You might not fall into that category, but how many times have you intended to 'just quickly buy your daughter a few books on Amazon', only to have your attention diverted to another website, and then to another, only to realise that you've spent the last hour mindlessly browsing the web? With so many apps around, there are actually apps to help you stay off apps (yes, that's right!). Shop around and find one that's ideal for you. There are several cool features such as blocking apps at designated hours, measuring the time spent on your smartphone, annoying alerts to remind you it's already been 30 minutes since you've logged on to your social media account, and more!

2. Take advantage of wait times. Someone's late for a meeting, there's a queue at the checkout line, you're waiting at the doctor's clinic, or at the school pickup. Treat this time with care and use it to read (the Kindle and the Kindle app which sync automatically with the Kindle itself is great for this!), take a crossword puzzle, or do anything which can be done on the run!

3. Have a lunch break self-care regimen. If skipping your lunch break is not an option, try scheduling one lunch break a week for some self-care. You can get some exercise done, do some shopping for yourself, get a manicure or mini-massage, read, or even fit in a quick trip to the hairdresser.

4. Make bedtimes 'mama times'. We've already mentioned the importance of getting the kids to bed early for their sake—what we have not mentioned is how important this is for your sanity! Dedicate as little time as possible to preparing for the next day and clearing up, and from then onwards, relax. This is your time!

5. Wake up earlier. This doesn't work for everyone, but if you're a morning person, this will work a treat! Use 15 extra minutes to have a mindful cup of tea, or 20 minutes to do some meditation or yoga. If you can afford some more, go for a quick jog! Several people swear by adjusting their bedtime to an earlier time and training themselves to get up earlier. They say the early bird catches the worm and this is so true! In the evening, decision fatigue kicks in and you find yourself dragging your feet in utter exhaustion. All you want to do is hit the bed and sleep! So many successful people wake up incredibly early and make the most of the morning hours. Michelle Obama, Avon Products CEO Andrea Jung, Vogue Editor-in-Chief Anna Wintour, and Starbucks President Michelle Gass are all very early risers, to name a few.

What to do in your free time

Now that you've managed to make some well-deserved time for yourself, be intentional, and use your time wisely.

Exercise

De-stressing, mood enhancing, calorie-burning, body-toning— the benefits are endless. You may choose to make time for yourself to exercise. You needn't sign up for a gym member-ship or classes if you aren't up for it. A quick jog can make you feel revitalised. Reward yourself by allowing yourself to listen to your favourite podcast while exercising.

Read

Find a little corner in your house or in your area and make this your reading spot. Make it special and choose somewhere away from the mayhem where you can get lost in a few good pages. Think simple: the little corner in your balcony on a comfy chair, in your bed with the lights dimmed, or on the bench in the alley behind your house.

Learn

With the internet at our fingertips it's so easy to learn new skills, such as gardening, sketching, cooking exotic food, or editing photos. Read online, look for how-to videos on You-Tube, and buy any tools you need to get started. Finally, prac-tise! You never know when you might come across a new hobby!

Watch a TV series

Catch on to whatever's popular and join in the excited chats on social media or between friends whenever a new episode is on. Not quite as productive as the other suggestions but you might be the type to find this enjoyable! After all, we're otherwise productive beings around the clock!

Pamper yourself

Prepare a nice, warm bath with some essential oils, light a few candles, put on some soft music, and take some time out in the bath. Treat yourself to a nice body scrub and a face mask.

Breathe

Something as simple as breathing effectively combats stress and activates the body's natural response to stress. The 4-7-8 breathing technique is very simple to learn and do. Try it, and keep it up for two weeks, and see how better you feel!

The 4-7-8 breathing technique involves the following:

1. Relax your tongue so the tip is touching the place where the back of your top teeth meet the roof of your mouth.
2. Exhale completely.
3. Close your mouth.
4. Inhale through your nose for 4 seconds.
5. Hold for 7 seconds.
6. Exhale for 8 seconds.

Common happiness stumbling blocks

Life sure is complicated, so the points hereunder are surely not the *only* stress-inducing issues which you might be facing. That said, most of these points are a common denominator amongst mamas.

1. Babies and free time

When you have a baby, all your free time vanishes in thin air. Babies thrive on close physical contact and need their mum for survival. They require constant love and attention. This is especially true if you have a clingy baby. It gets better, and your baby will not be as needy forever. Enjoy the moment while it lasts, as it is very short-lived.

2. Not getting enough sleep

Try not to fall into this trap. Ease your body into a bedtime routine by starting to wind down at a decent hour every night. Create a simple, calming regimen such as: shower, chamomile tea, one TV episode, and into bed for some reading. Whatever you do, do not fall asleep in front of the TV!

3. Kids sleeping late

It's common knowledge that kids of different ages need different hours of sleep. It's surprising how much they actually need. If your kids are young (6 and under), start moving their bedtime routine 15 minutes backwards every day until you reach the desired bedtime. In the case of older kids, you will probably get a complaint or two, but be firm and instigate.

SOUND ADVICE

Kids start getting out of hand once they start getting tired, and it is so important that they are tucked in before they get to this point. The fact that they are tucked in also pushes you to start getting things done and get your bedtime routine started.

4. Kids sharing your bed

I know that there are mixed feelings about co-sleeping; personally, I'm all for it whilst a baby is still a newborn, and then all against. One simple reason is that it is perfectly normal for babies to make noises while they're asleep, and for them to wake up, cry for a few seconds, and go back to sleep. If they're in the same bed as us, more often than not, we're the ones waking them. Another reason is that, sometimes, kids get so attached that they're still co-sleeping when they're toddlers, and then it's so hard to get them to sleep in their bedroom!

5. Aiming for perfection

Perfect house, perfect body, perfect this, perfect that. Do not aim for perfect, aim for good enough. There is no such thing as perfect, and aiming for something unattainable will only make you miserable.

6. Taking on too much

You need to seriously think about the time you actually have available before committing yourself to anything else. This is especially true in relation to kids' activities. Limit the kids to one extracurricular activity each per week. Try to combine them into a day or two if possible. It's easier if you're out of the house one or two full days, rather than going in and out most of the week. Carpool with a friend or two, if at all possible.

7. Stressing yourself out

Use logical sense to truly weigh the seriousness of a situation. Try to take yourself out of the picture. When you're overwhelmed, you're bound to see everything as being far worse than it is. Stressing will not help solve anything. Remember, it was the last straw that broke the camel's back.

LOOKING GOOD

I'm sure you all know how to make yourself look not just good, but fabulous, but understandably, it takes a tad bit more effort to look good when you're a mum. In between literally being thrown up on, to using up all your energy by juggling your kid's million and one needs, you might not think you have the time or cannot be bothered to look good.

Beauty hacks for the busy mum

You will love the following tips and tricks that are bound to keep you looking in tip-top shape by taking a few simple, well-thought-out steps!

Make sure your hair looks good

Once your hair looks good, you look so much more put together!

- Get a good haircut. Opt for something low maintenance, depending on your hair type.

- Prolong a hair wash by applying dry shampoo before going to bed, and possibly when you wake up.

- If you have a bad hair day, or your hair needs a wash and you can't afford to wash it on the day, opt for a stylish messy bun, a side part, or posh looking low ponytail.

- Find a hairdresser that will come to your home to save yourself time and money, and to have no issues with who will be watching the kids.

Your face

- Keep to a simple routine of cleansing and moisturising every morning and night, but keep perfume-free makeup remover wipes as a backup for when you can't be bothered. It's OK!

- Buy moisturiser with SPF to double as a sunblock.

- Puffy eyes? Boil some water, dip in two teabags, let them cool slightly, and put them over your eyes for five minutes. Magic!

- Add a touch of makeup. If you're short on time, mascara, some blusher, and lip gloss will breathe life back into your face!

Your hands & feet

- Keep hand cream at your desk or workspace. Make a habit of applying whilst you are waiting for someone to answer your call.

- Keep your nails a short enough length to avoid breakage.

- After applying nail polish, dip your nails in cold water to help set the polish.

- If you can afford to, find a nail technician (there are many who do house visits) to apply gel nail polish every three weeks. It does not budge and needs to be completely removed before being reapplied.

- Before you go to bed, apply body lotion to your feet and put on a pair of cotton socks. You will wake up with the softest feet! The same applies to your hands when using a pair of cotton gloves. Try it out!

- Always use rubber gloves when cleaning, especially when you are using chemical products.

STYLE & WARDROBE

I know many women who have so many clothes but still insist they have *nothing* to wear. Are you one of them? The problem does not lie within your clothes but your shopping habits, instincts, and decision-making skills.

What not to do

Here are some major blunders:

1. You're holding on to clothes which should be put aside

Clothes which do not fit well, or have gone out of style, should be donated. It's time to get real. Any pieces in your closet that do not fit well *now* should not be in your closet at all. It's useless holding on to jeans that fit so well three years and six kilos ago. They will only make you sad every time you look at them, making you wish you still had that slimmer body. Instead, concentrate on the clothes that make you feel fabulous now. If you have just recently had a baby and are still losing the baby weight, allow yourself some time before discarding any smaller-sized clothes.

2. You're shopping blindly

You might be picking out items that you love and adore and are so pretty they make you smile, but are you shopping with an outfit in mind? Every piece of clothing you buy must at least be easily paired with three items from your closet. If not, it will hang there sadly until the day comes when you realise that you are not wearing it, and it's probably become outdated.

3. You have a lot of trendy pieces and not enough basics

Talk about over-inspired! Whilst it is fun and really great that you experiment and enjoy shopping new trends, not having enough basics to pair them with is as big a problem as not having anything at all in your closet. Make sure your closet has all the basics required so you can mix and match that funky new blazer you just got and can wear it to death before it goes out of style!

4. You own too many clothes

This is the result of one or more of the above. If you own so much, everything is crammed, and you definitely do not have room to hang up the majority of your clothes. If you can hang it, do so, your clothes will be more visible. If you can't see it, you can't wear it!

5. Your clothes don't reflect your lifestyle

The lifestyle you led ten years ago is probably very different from the lifestyle you lead today. Reflect on how you spend your days and buy clothes according to what you need. If out of the 16 hours you spend awake you spend eight at work, and eight at home, your wardrobe should contain mostly that.

If you can manage to buy pieces that can migrate from your work wardrobe to your weekend wardrobe, all the better. A great example is a pretty blouse, worn with smart trousers or skirts for the office, and casual jeans for the weekend.

6. You keep buying the same item over and over

You might adore floral shirts, but having more than one or two will *really* make you feel like you really have nothing to wear. Try to have variety in your closet. Hang similar pieces next to each other to ensure that you do not get stuck in this rut.

Figuring out your ideal wardrobe in 2 easy steps

Step 1: When it comes to your style, decide what your priority is

You might want to buy cheap but decent clothes or you might prefer a capsule wardrobe. Some enjoy trying the latest trends, whilst others enjoy neutrals and basics.

Figure out what you would like to have in your closet. Think about what matters to you. If it's style you're after, saving money will have to take a backseat, and most probably it will take a little longer to get dressed in the morning, at least until you get into the groove of things.

If you're into budget-conscious dressing, you might have to do some more research and shop the sales wisely to find items within your reach which also look good on you.

Once you know what your priority is, it is a little easier to shop since you now know what matters to you the most.

Step 2: Ask yourself—How do I want to feel in my clothes?

This simple question can help you get to the bottom of what you should be wearing. If your outfits do not match how you want to feel, you will not feel good in your clothes. If you want to feel comfortable, it's useless wearing stiletto heels; if you want to feel well put-together, wearing joggers will not help; and if you want to feel accomplished, jeans and t-shirts will not do the job!

Really think about how you want to feel, and dress the part.

SOUND ADVICE

You cannot just buy clothes because they fit, or because they're cheap, and they look OK. Buy only things which will make you feel exactly how you want to feel.

Have fun with this! Think about who you want to be and start dressing the part.

A few styling tips

1. Get rid of clothes that you don't love

Do it gradually, you cannot rid yourself of 80% of your clothes and end up with nothing. Invest in items that you adore and that check off all the boxes, and eliminate your not-so-favourite things out of your closet until you end up with a wardrobe that you love.

2. Have a uniform

Having a uniform is not literally wearing the identical same item over and over. This essentially means that you define a combination of clothing items to fit your style and to eliminate having lots of decisions to make. For example, you might be a polo shirt and jeans girl during the weekend and a dresses and heels girl for the office. You can also have 'uniforms' specific to the days of the week. If you're running to meetings on Tuesdays, your Tuesday uniform can be a pant or dress suit, if Wednesday is the day you run errands after work, your Wednesday uniform would ideally consist of comfortable shoes, so flats, classic jeans and a shirt would work out perfectly.

3. Not everything suits everyone

No matter how much you might love something, if it doesn't suit you, cross it off your list. Always choose clothing pieces in which you look great because that will make you feel great!

4. Invest in basics

Buy well-made and well-fitting pieces which you will wear over and over, and outlive all your trendy pieces. Invest in classic jeans, perfect black trousers, a little black dress, a leather jacket, a trench coat, a white shirt, a white t-shirt, and so on. Splurge a little more on these items, so they do not start fading or losing shape from the frequent wearing and washing.

4. Spend a little less on the trendier stuff

Trends rarely last more than two to three seasons, and who wants to empty their wallet on a blouse that will not get worn more than a couple of times?

5. Accessorise

Spend a little on a few of each of the following: winter scarves, lighter scarves or pashminas, earrings, bracelets, necklaces, and hats. Opt for different styles and colours. An interesting accessory will make an outfit stand out!

Don't forget that the importance of decluttering applies to your wardrobe as well.

A clothing item that you *might need* for a certain occasion, or *might* wear if you lose some kilos does not deserve space in your wardrobe. Do you reach for these items? No. Get rid of these things in your closet. Don't keep them if they don't work for you. They don't deserve space in your closet.

> ## SOUND ADVICE
>
> *Whatever you wear, remember that you are beautiful. Do not wait until you find and put on the perfect outfit to feel beautiful. It is not about the clothes. It's about you! Clothes are there to simply complement your already beautiful self!*

Tips for getting dressed in the morning

Before kids come on to the scene, getting dressed and looking great every day was a breeze.

Factor the kids in, and lo and behold, you probably lack your usual style and wear a lot of the same.

Whilst this does not bother everyone, it might bother you. If you are the type who enjoys dressing up and looking good, you will undoubtedly enjoy the following tips and steps:

1. The first thing you should do as soon as the younger kids are in bed is choose your outfit for the next day.

2. Choose wisely. Take a look at your weather app on your phone to see what the weather will look like. Wind + floaty skirt + heels + parking one road away from nursery school, or suede shoes + beige trousers + rain are not ideal combos.

3. Be creative. Utilise your wardrobe. Look at your clothes, try to wear pieces which you have not worn for a while and

incorporate them into a different outfit.

4. Hang the next day's outfit somewhere handy, and next to it lay out any accessories or jewellery you plan to wear with it.

5. Next, choose a matching handbag. It can be a downright pain in the backside to change your handbag daily. If you carry around quite a bit, which is probably the case, the mere thought of transferring all your stuff into another handbag is tiring in itself. This is where the indispensable handbag organiser comes in. All your essentials are packed into this handy bag which goes into your handbag. Now changing your handbag takes seconds!

6. The shoes. Choose the pair you will be wearing and place them next to the door, in your entryway or wherever is most handy. Remember to clean and place that day's pair back in their place. Everyone's shoes should also go next to the door so everyone can get their shoes on as you are all leaving the house.

7. Jackets/hats/scarves and all outerwear (this also applies to the whole family) should be placed strategically next to the door. If you have space for hooks or a coat hanger next to the door, do yourself a favour and get one installed.

KEY POINTS

1. All mums experience guilty feelings. If it's not because you are a working mum, it's because you take time out for yourself, and if it's not because you take time out for yourself, it's because you are trying so hard to be perfect.

2. Self-care is vital and will ultimately make you a better person and mother.

3. Make time for yourself and dedicate it to a hobby, indulgent entertainment or relaxation.

4. Looking good everyday does not mean you need to spend too much time preening yourself.

5. Being well-dressed is synonymous with understanding what works for you and figuring out what you want to wear.

CHAPTER 9
RELATIONSHIP GOALS

"Relationships are valuable no matter who they are between."
—Donna Goddard
Waldmeer

RELATIONSHIPS: THE ULTIMATE HAPPINESS BOOSTER

Great relationships with those around you are synonymous with happiness, and people and socialising are a definite happiness booster.

With limited spare time on your hands you might be guilty of not giving much thought to relationships in general.

Be it your spouse, partner, children, parents, siblings, workmates, best friends, or childhood friends, you can find ways and means to stay in touch and keep that relationship alive and thriving.

Why you should invest in people

1. Relationships are essential. The happiest and healthiest people all pursue strong relationships with people they trust and enjoy spending time with.

2. Psychologists have found that people are happier when they are in the company of others (as opposed to alone), and this rings true for both introverts and extroverts.

3. Your fast-paced life is busy and keeps you happy and on your toes, but once your kids grow up and are less dependent on you, friendships will take on a more important role.

4. Having a network of close family and friends means you will have a support system in times of need.

Keeping your relationships alive and well

Watch your greetings

Always express your happiness when you see someone, be it with a bright smile and a hello, a warm hug, or a kiss. Give the person a second or two to make them feel appreciated, and always part with a sound goodbye.

Stop for a second

Multitasking is great, but a minute or two of your time won't make a difference to your day. If a colleague stops by to say hello, stop what you're doing and exchange some pleasant chit-chat. If your kids need to tell you something, put down your kitchen knife, face them, and give them your full attention.

Be responsive

If you receive an email or a message, acknowledge the person on the other end. Do not procrastinate. A short reply is better than no reply at all. If you keep putting it off because you want to send a long reply, hours turn into days, and days turn into weeks, and before you know it, you're losing touch.

SOUND ADVICE

Say hello. A quick SMS, online chat, email—anything short and sweet lets someone else know you are thinking of them, however busy you are.

'Save' your favourite people

Create a favourites list on your smartphone and add all your closest loved ones and friends. Getting in touch with your dearest and nearest will take seconds, and lack of communication with someone particular will stand out when you see their names on your list.

Compliment

Everyone likes compliments, and complimenting someone on an achievement or their looks will make them feel motivated, noticed, and appreciated.

Reach out

If someone close to you is going through a tough time, just acknowledging their sadness and extending your heartfelt support can make a world of difference.

PRACTICAL WAYS TO HELP DIFFERENT RELATIONSHIPS THRIVE

Your children

"Your children need your presence, more than your presents."

—Jesse Jackson

We are so focused on making sure our children get everything that they need, that time flies before our eyes and we fail to mindfully plan occasions or opportunities to work on our relationship with them.

Create a closer connection with your child by putting your love into action on a day-to-day basis.

Read together
Reading books to your children, or reading together in very close proximity each evening is a smart way to bond with your little ones.

Participate
This is especially true for older children. Take the time and interest to spend time doing something they love. It might be an art class, a computer game, or watching sports. Merely trying to understand why they love what they do shows them a lot of love.

Spend time with them every day
Little children are more of a no-brainer. Being needier, one cannot but drop everything and partake in a few games. Once your kids get older, and are pretty much independent, one has to really prioritise to make this happen. Spend at least a few mindful minutes a day with your kid, even if you just sit with them before they go to sleep, talk to them, and then tuck them in.

Schedule fun dates together
Stick this into your diary, and once a month organise something fun together. If you're married or in a relationship, forget about your better half and make this about you and your kids. It might be as simple as baking a cake or going for a drive

in the rain and singing loudly to your favourite songs. Better yet, in summer, when your kids are on holiday, organise 'Fun Fridays' and do something together each week.

Your family

Family is those around whom you can be yourself and in whom you can find refuge in times of need. Staying connected with your relatives will give you a sense of belonging, love, and security.

- Geographical distance is no longer an issue with all the technological advances made in the last few years. Schedule Skype dates, share family photos over email, and keep up with one's life experiences on social media.

- If you have extended family who live close to you, plan to have dinner together once a week. You can take turns to meet at each other's houses. There's no need for have a fancy affair—just cook what you would have cooked, but for more people, or get take-out.

- If possible, make it a point to organise a family lunch or coffee date for each other's birthdays. It needn't fall on the same day as the birthday, as long as you all come together to wish the person a happy birthday and spend time with each other in a joyful atmosphere.

- Hold on to traditions, be it an annual Easter egg hunt, beginning of summer barbecue, or ordering in for New Year's Eve. Traditions give you and those involved a warm feeling of belonging.

- Support each other. If your aunt is in hospital, take it in turns to visit. Sister had a baby? Organise to take over some home-made food. Show your family members that you genuinely care.

The husband, partner, or romantic interest

If you're married or in a steady relationship, take your time to appreciate each other. Try not to fall into the trap of letting the days rush by without spending a few authentic moments with each other to express your emotions.

If you're dating, enjoy it, and make time for it! Nothing gives you a boost like a flirtatious date.

Have a small gift on hand
This can be a favourite chocolate, a book, a sweet card—anything inexpensive but thoughtful will do. Nothing shows appreciation like a thoughtful gift delivered at the perfect moment!

Plan quality time with your better half
The days fly by, and not being intentional about this is a big no-no. Choose one day or night a week to dedicate to your better half.

Date your husband
This can be as simple as putting the kids to bed and having a glass of wine and a few nibbles together or cuddling up on the sofa to watch a movie.

Go out and have fun
If you have family nearby, let your kids sleep over once in a while and spend a night out together. If you have friends with

kids your age, take it in turns to watch the kids every other week. Get a sitter if need be! Think about going out on an afternoon date, and coming back home for the kids' bedtime so you may enjoy an extended date at home (sneaky!).

Talk

This one seems easy, but think about the last time you gave your partner or spouse your full attention and asked how they were. Make it a point to intentionally ask how their day was, or if they need any help, every single day.

Show some love

At least once a day, show your better half you love them in some way, shape, or form. Send a sweet SMS halfway through the day, write 'I love you' on the bathroom mirror, put a note in their lunch bag, or make them coffee whilst they shower.

Your friends

SOUND ADVICE

A loving relationship cannot and should not substitute friendship. Friends are more important than we might think.

- Pick one day a week to spend 15 minutes texting or chatting with your friends. It might be as simple as sending an SMS with, *"Hey, how are you? I've had a busy week, but I've been thinking of you!"*

- Schedule a lunch date, coffee, or outing at least once a month. If you can afford to do it more often, do so! This needs to go into your diary. Either opt for a set date every month, say the first Saturday of the month, or else, every time you meet up with your friends, plan the following month's meetup.

- Too busy? Have an errand date. Catch up with your friend whilst running errands together. This is a brilliant multi-tasking hack that is also environmentally friendly!

- Exercise together. If you live reasonably close, attend a class together, or go for a brisk walk around the block. If you have no one to watch the kids, take them with you!

Your workmates

Being happy at work definitely means getting along with your co-workers. Cheery good mornings and loud office banter can and will make your day brighter.

Here's how to strengthen those work ties:

- Make them tea! Nothing shows love like a round of tea or coffee for your workmates!

- Have a break. Sometimes we all need to get away from our monitors for two minutes of air. Stop by a co-worker's desk and ask them how their day is going.

- Stop and enjoy. Yes, we are all for getting stuff done during our breaks, but once in a while do forget about your to-do list and have your lunch break with your colleagues.

- Buy some biscuits. Or nuts. Or chocolate. Everyone appreciates a little something delicious once in a while!

- Have an 'office series'. It is so much fun to all watch a particular TV show and be able to talk excitedly about who did what every week!

JUST DATING

SOUND ADVICE

Dating is fun! It can take the pressure off your day-to-day whirlwind life. So if you're a single mum and you haven't already—get dating, and enjoy yourself!

A few dating do's and don'ts

DO be honest about your intentions. You might be looking for a casual fling, or long-term romance—whatever it is, be upfront. It's OK to have different mindsets, just as long as you are honest about it.

DON'T introduce your date too quickly to your children. It can be very confusing and heart-wrenching for kids, especially those craving a father figure in their lives, to have someone disappear into the sunset after they have become a part of their lives. If he or she is asking to meet your kids a tad too early, explain why you need to take it slow and be absolutely sure your relationship is there for the long haul before you take the next step.

DO keep the talk about your past to a minimum. Don't scare your date off with horror stories about your ex or your break up. Your past love life should not be the subject of your date, ever.

DON'T feel guilty. Do not even think about letting guilt creep into your farthest thoughts. It's OK to spend time away from your children for your pure, unadulterated pleasure. You deserve to have the time to date and the potential to meet someone who deserves you!

DO find someone reliable to watch your kids. You do not want to spend the night or afternoon worrying if your kids are in good hands. Take it in turns with friends who have kids the same age, ask family to watch your kids, or ask around for a reliable babysitter.

DON'T talk constantly about the kids. Your children should not be the topic of the night.

Re-entering the dating world

Dating is always tricky and is definitely a challenge and a scary place to be *until* you get your groove back.

Follow these pointers to help you get back into the game:

1. Go online

The majority of today's trends are online, and so is dating. There are several dating apps available, and you can take your time to chat with someone from the comfort of your own home before you decide to meet up.

2. Do something new

If you do not want to or do not have the time to take up a new hobby or class, do something as simple as going for a coffee at a nearby coffee shop during your lunch hour. New places equal new faces.

3. Blind date

Be warned! Only partake in this if you have friends you trust with your life and they can truly recommend someone you will like. Should this be the case, this can be one of the best ways to meet someone new, as no one knows you better than your bestie.

4. Enjoy yourself!

Relax, and enjoy the experience. It's important not to go into dating with a fixation on meeting the right one. Stay open-minded and you never know what might happen!

WHEN YOUR SOCIAL LIFE IS A THING OF THE PAST

Rekindling friendships

Don't feel bad if you are guilty of letting go of past friendships.

Unless you feel like you cannot relate to your friends any longer (which is another thing altogether), this might be due to the fact that you tried to juggle more than you could handle and ended up dropping the ball.

If you genuinely miss an old friend with whom you have lost touch, you can always reach out and try to make amends.

Reviving an old friendship is possible, and if you feel you had a bond with someone, they probably feel the same way.

How to do it:

1. **Reach out.** There's no need to jump right in and call someone out of the blue to ask them to meet. Take things step by step. Send a casual text or chat message to ask how they are, and start making amends.

2. **Keep in touch.** Social media is a great way to make very casual connections with someone. Like their photos, make a joke or two, or comment on the content that they share.

3. **Make a date.** If you seem to be making headway, ask that person to meet up for a coffee.

4. **Open up and be honest.** There's nothing shameful about trying so hard that you fail in some way or another. Your friend will understand, especially if she is a true friend, and even more so if she is a mother.

5. **Keep it up.** Now that you've come this far, keep making time for your friend.

Reaching out

Never feel like you're too old to make new friends. On the contrary, as I've found out from experience, making friends when you're older is an exhilarating and fun experience. Why?

1. You are more confident and only allow the real you to shine through.

2. Hence, you attract like-minded people.

3. You do not take any nonsense and instantly shy away from fake or toxic friendships.

4. For the most part, peer pressure is less of a big deal.

5. Your increased confidence as an adult also allows you to make friends easier than when you were younger.

How to make new friends

The number one piece of advice I can offer you is to be practical and to try to make friends who lead a similar lifestyle to your own or with whom you appear to have some things in common. Trying to make a new friend who lives on the other side of town, is childless, works super-long hours, *and* goes for post-office drinks three times a week is probably not a good idea in that it will be a tad difficult to make plans without a lot of effort.

Instead, try one (or all!) of the following:

- Say hello to someone in your town or village. Neighbours can make terrific friends!

- Make chit-chat with another mum from your child's school.

- If you attend a fitness class, or your kids attend a sports club or other extracurricular activity, it's an ideal place to meet like-minded mums.

More quick tips

Say cheese!
Be approachable and smile. Say hello to people who appear to be receptive to your friendliness.

Chat away
Make small talk. It's so much easier to break the ice if you're connecting with another mum, and especially if your kids have something in common, or they are playing together.

Plan a play date (or a coffee date)
Once you get chatting and if you feel at ease with the person, plan to meet up with the kids and bond whilst the kids play. In all honesty, using the children as an excuse to meet up works wonders in this case, because if you realise at some point that you are not into the person you are meeting, no pressure is put on either one of you. If you feel brave enough to ask someone you do not know to meet up for a coffee (sans kids, in the event that the person you have in mind is not a mother), good on you, girl!

Keep in touch
Use the tips listed in this chapter to stay connected to your new friend!

KEY POINTS

1. Relationships and people are the basis of happiness.

2. You can create a closer connection with those around you by being intentional and present in a few simple ways.

3. If you're single–date! It's fun, and you never know who you might meet!

4. It's OK to have been 'careless' with past friendships; it's possible to reach out and rekindle what you once had.

CHAPTER 10
LET'S HAVE SOME FUN, MUM!

"Travel, in the younger sort, is a part of education; in the elder, a part of the experience."
—Francis Bacon

Vacations, birthdays, gifting, playing hostess, throwing birthday parties–yikes! Do not panic! All this can sound rather daunting but can be dealt with easily and efficiently if you plan ahead. A LOT of this can be done online and can save you tons of running around, headaches and money.

Let's start with vacations.

As parents, we count down the days to holidays so we can recharge our batteries and get the opportunity to kick back and relax. We also crave new experiences and dream of visiting new locations and learning about different cultures.

Vacation types

A vacation needn't be long, expensive, or far away from home. Simply switching off and forgetting about your daily responsibilities for a few days whilst enjoying yourself and your family is a holiday in itself.

Here are a few ideas for simple holidays.

1. Being a tourist in your own city

Plan a few days' holiday in your own hometown or city. Clear your calendar for a few days and enjoy being a tourist. Enjoy the days leading up to your holiday; make a countdown and research the best sites and restaurants for your break. When the big day arrives, get into the tourist mindset. That means no cleaning, no laundry, and no errands! Carrying a camera everywhere you go will help you get into the groove of things and will make for some great memories!

2. Visit a nearby town/village/island

Your country is a rich, varied territory with so many great options which are a short drive or ferry ride away. Make the most of it! Plan a day trip or a few days' break, or organise a fun road trip with stops in different locations.

3. Go camping

Camping is so much fun, and a fantastic way to spend quality time with your family. Sleeping in such close proximity, building campfires, cooking together, huddling up in the cold evening and roasting marshmallows…

If you're unsure if camping is for you, you can easily rent tents at a campsite together with access to showers, a grocery store, electricity, and a few more 'luxuries' for a very decent price.

4. The weekend break

Keep your eyes and ears wide open for hotel deals. If you come across a great deal, and the hotel is located reasonably close, go for it! Just having a clean room to sleep in, beds made every day, and a nice breakfast to wake up to will make you feel refreshed! The best offers include half board or full board dining. Take a book or two, some toys for the kids, swimsuits (weather dependent, unless the hotel has an indoor pool) and a card game or board game if your kids are older, and indulge in some well-earned time off.

THE MORE ELABORATE HOLIDAYS

Planning a trip

Keep your eyes and ears open for trip ideas. Ask around. Add various trip ideas to your bucket list as they land into your lap! Pinterest is very handy for this, as are numerous websites, forums, social media pages, and podcasts.

The following are some tips to get you going:

1. Plan ahead

Planning ahead is key and will give you ample time to sort out everything to the last detail. If planning a holiday is not your cup of tea, and is your husband's, partner's, or friend's, take the opportunity to delegate.

2. Involving the kids in the planning process is a great idea!

It might take longer to get to the end line; however, a holiday can be so much easier on everyone if the kids are involved as they can feel like they have more control over what's going on.

If you're not up to this, try to make them feel like they made some of the decisions by giving them a few options which, in reality, are insignificant, such as picking one restaurant or the other, when they would like to visit a particular sight, and so on. You saying, *"Great idea, this is SO much fun!"*, is so much more pleasant than having to drag a sulky and displeased kid from one sight to another.

3. Use an online map, such as Google Maps

Google Maps is a fantastic tool! Save all your favourite spots on an online map and code according to type. Let's say you'd like to mark a few restaurants you want to try, a couple of museums, and your favourite shopping mall. You can very easily use a fork and knife icon for the restaurants, a museum icon for museums, and shopping bags for the shopping mall. It is also very simple to measure distances and make a sensible plan since it is very easy to visualise everything on the map.

The saved map can be shared with family members and fellow travellers, and everyone can add and edit to their heart's desires.

ORGANISATION TIP

When adding a 'pin' to mark a spot on Google Maps, take note of the coordinates in the notes section of the pin. This will come in handy when you are on holiday—all you need to do is enter the coordinates into your GPS and off you go!

4. Pre-book where possible

Some major sights offer a separate, faster queue for people who pre-book their tickets online. Do your homework and check out the sights you plan to visit before you go.

5. Busy days out, early nights in (or easy nights out)

Plan to have fun packed days from the moment your kids are up, when they are well rested and up for adventure. Ideally, to minimise stress as much as possible, you should base yourself in an area where you can easily walk to a few shops and restaurants in the evening.

If you are opting for an accommodation which is not quite central, you have two options: either spend a full day out and return after an early dinner, or else, if the accommodation is self-catering or offers a half-board option, have dinner back at your choice of lodging. Don't stress yourself out with cooking though—buy something that can be easily heated up or a selection of fresh bread, cheeses, and local delicacies to enjoy!

6. Book an apartment

This tip makes so much sense, even more so if you have kids under the age of five, or kids of different age groups with different bedtimes. We always book an apartment when we holiday.

Our daughter, aged three, has a much earlier bedtime than her 12-year-old brother, and by early evening she is always exhausted from taking in so many new things all day long. With an apartment, we can put her down to sleep in one of the bedrooms and not worry about the rest of us. I can take my time unpacking and re-packing bags for the next day, and my husband and I can also spend some quality time together when both kids hit the sack!

You can always do with the extra space that comes with an apartment too!

When to holiday

The ideal time depends on your priorities.

If your children are school-aged, chances are your priority is to travel when the children are on holiday, so that pretty much restricts most of the months for travel.

Another priority might be a low-budget holiday; however this is harder to source combined with holidaying when school is out.

If you are travelling when school is out you still have plenty of options, including long weekends, Easter, Christmas, mid-term, or summer holidays. Planning and booking in advance are definitely recommended. This will save you some money because both flights and accommodation are cheaper when there is decent availability, as well as having more options will give you access to the more competitive options.

Your child might be passing through a phase of getting sick on a regular basis, and if this is the case, travelling during summer will automatically mean there is less chance of having to cancel, or worse, your child getting sick on holiday.

In the case of travelling during the summer holidays, always check that the main sights and shops are open in the case of countries such as Italy, where a lot of businesses shut down in August for Ferragosto.

Looking for low-budget travel?

Most likely, you will need to travel during low season for the very best deals. The more flexible you are, the better deals you will be able to get in terms of flights and accommodation. Of course, this comes with its downsides, starting from the weather. Snow, rain, monsoons, and extreme cold might be off-putting. In the case of most destinations, off-season travel equals shorter days. Some businesses may also be shut down during this period and major sights might be under construction. Children's sights or parks as well as theme parks, playgrounds, and zoos will most probably be closed.

Transport may be somewhat limited, bus and train services are scaled back, and ferries do not operate due to rough seas.

Travelling off-peak also carries its advantages, of which the most obvious are prices. Flights and accommodation are much cheaper, not to mention the wider availability due to lesser traffic. The crowds are considerably less and getting into museums is a breeze. The overall trip is much calmer, and kids are easier to manage when there is more room to breathe and less chance of losing sight of them in an instant. Customer service is usually at its best in the quieter times of the year. With hotels, restaurants, sights and transportation being substantially less busy, staff everywhere is under less pressure and stress so they can offer a better level of service. You and your kids get to enjoy everybody's full attention wherever you go.

Automatically, having fewer tourists around gives you more chance to mingle with the locals and immerse yourself in the new culture. The locals might actually be more eager to engage with you, given that they are not overwhelmed with the influx of tourists.

SOUND ADVICE

Several apps, such as Skyscanner offer the huge benefit of colour coding all the days on the calendar according to the price bracket they fall under. You can easily select the cheapest days to travel on since they are marked in, let's say, green, which saves you lots of time looking up different dates. Alerts can help you stay on top of pricing decreases or increases.

Where to go

The sky's the limit! Besides being spoilt for choice in terms of location, there are also a wide array of holiday options and styles to choose from.

First adventures

Start off small, or better yet, take along some extended family members such as the grandparents for an extra hand. Family members can make a holiday a much more relaxed one as they can watch your little ones while you have a shower and get dressed in peace, take them for a buggy ride or walk if they get bored, or accompany them to the loo if they are potty trained. Grandparents, in particular, will be over the moon if invited on a family holiday together with their grandkids. This option works out for everyone!

Cruising

Some holidays are better suited for travel with babies or little kids.

An all-inclusive cruise, especially one departing from a close locality is the ultimate lay-back-and-enjoy-the-experience kind of holiday. Whilst it is not such an adventurous option, it is surely a brilliant one when you already have a lot to think about when travelling with younger kids.

All you need to do is simply book in advance; everything is thought for—entertainment, day trips, tours, activities, dining, the works. Most cruise liners, particularly ones which cater for families, have terrific on-board activities for the kids as well as babysitting services for a well-deserved night out.

All-inclusive resorts also cater for all of the above and are particularly suited to a relaxing holiday when the children are little.

Seasoned travellers

Once you are well-adjusted to travelling with your wee ones you can opt for more bold adventures.

If you are travelling to countries that might require immunisations as a requirement, check with your local healthcare provider about the details such as how old the kids need to be to be able to take the shots and what the side effects are.

GETTING TO YOUR DESTINATION

There are a number of travel options to consider, depending on your destination, the weather, budget, and preferences. You generally may get to your destination using a car, plane, train, or another vehicle such as a caravan.

Cars and other vehicles

If you are able to fit in your family and suitcases into your car, and provided the destination of your choice is reachable by vehicle, travelling by car is a fantastic option when you have little kids under ten years of age.

SOUND ADVICE

Having full control of your journey can make travel less stressful. Bathroom breaks and lunch breaks may be taken as you please, and if the trip is on the longer side you may opt to stop at a guesthouse or B&B overnight to recharge your batteries before you set off again the next day.

The hard work when travelling by car is keeping the kids entertained and buckled in. Still, this is not nearly as half as stressful as flying.

I do have some tricks up my sleeve to keep your little ones from getting bored silly and moaning non-stop.

1. Tablet

We all know to stay away from too much screen time, but a holiday calls for bending the rules. Explain to your kids that you understand that the car ride is long, and they might get bored, therefore the rules do not apply on this occasion and they may watch a movie or two whilst travelling.

Choosing to give a tablet to one of your children only if they are acting up could backfire, in the sense that you could get repeat difficult behaviour once they realise they will get extra screen time for being unreasonable.

2. Get some surprises wrapped up

Visit a shop that sells inexpensive items such as the 'Euro Shop', or the 'Dollar Store' in the US, and buy your kids bits and pieces to play with in the car. Wrap them up in brown paper and every hour, hand one surprise to each kid. The surprises needn't be anything spectacular; the sheer fun of opening something every hour will keep your kids excited. You can also hide them in the nooks and crannies of the car, and have the children look for them.

3. Audiobooks

There are plenty of audiobooks available to keep the whole family entertained. Kids as young as three are more or less able to follow an audiobook aimed at children.

4. Games

Play simple games with them, such as 'I spy' or 'I'm going on a picnic'.

I'm sure you're all familiar with 'I spy'. This is adaptable to toddlers. Instead of saying *"I spy, with my little eye, something beginning with h"*, say *"I spy, with my little eye...hair!"*, and have your little one point at her hair.

'I'm going on a picnic' is also pretty easy to play. It is suitable for kids from about age five upwards as it is a combination of an alphabet and a memory game. The game starts with the first person saying, *"I'm going on a picnic and I'm taking apples"*. The next person has to remember what the first person said and add on a word starting with the next letter, for example: *"I'm going on a picnic and I'm taking apples and bananas"*. This goes on for as long as possible. People forgetting or making mistakes are out, and the last one standing wins!

Some tips for airplane rides

All of the above-mentioned tips may also be used for airplane trips. Obviously, in the case of audio books or movies, one would need to use headphones.

If your children are little, say ages one to three, buy some foam stickers and have them enjoy sticking all of them onto the airplane tray table or your arms.

Take a few printouts for them to colour in. Blu-tack is a sneaky way of ensuring that the paper does not fall off the tray!

Quick tips for travel

1. Always print out two copies of all your reservations and important documents. Keep one copy in a transparent folder in your carry-on or in your handbag, and spare copies in another carry-on.

2. Always include copies of all passports in both the folder and your suitcase.

3. Once you arrive at your destination, one batch of copies is best placed in your handbag and carried around with you.

4. Label all passports with the name & expiry date for easier reference.

5. Leave a spare set of house keys with family or with a neighbour in case of emergencies.

6. Try to leave your house clean and organised.

7. If you can manage to pre-plan a menu for the following week after you arrive, it will make for a much better welcome! What's even better is having food in the freezer for at least the first three days. This will give you time to settle in without having to think about food.

8. Unless you arrive back home in the morning, having the next day off from work would be ideal. If you have a partner or husband, either one of you can stay home to at least unpack, sort out the laundry, and get back into the routine.

9. Think about safety in practical ways. Buy your kids travel I.D. bracelets and write down your phone number on

them. Have the family wear bright colours when visiting a busy city. Teach your kids that if lost, they should always look for a police officer, and if they cannot see any, they should ask a woman with children for help.

10. If you have young kids in a stroller, always carry a small chain and a padlock with you. This will definitely be a God-send should you wish to engage in an activity where your stroller cannot be taken on, such as a boat or bicycle ride; or if you are visiting an amusement park.

11. Tie a colourful ribbon or fabric to your suitcases. It will be easier to spot on the conveyer belt at the airport.

Out and about

Certain outings are better suited to children, especially in the case of babies and toddlers. As a rule of thumb, I always try to plan outings during the day, so as not to disrupt my youngest's sleep. Arriving back home at a late hour, and having your child wake up from a deep sleep when you try to put them to bed is no fun!

This does not mean that we never go out in the evenings, but daytime outings are less stressful and more fun for everyone!

Outing quick tips

1. Adapt according to the weather

If it's scorching hot avoid running around at peak hours or choose somewhere air conditioned in the afternoon. Always pack sunblock and mosquito repelling bands or stickers.

Do not let bad weather faze you, but think ahead in terms of practicality. If it is pouring, try to opt for someplace with underground parking, or somewhere reasonably accessible where parking is not that much of an issue.

2. Have your baby ready for bed

In the case of outings which last till bedtime, make sure your little one is wearing something comfortable that he or she can sleep in. Put your baby to sleep in his or her clothes, and do not disrupt them from a good night's sleep!

3. ...or prepare for bed on the go

Pack your child's pyjamas and cosy housecoat into a bag, and take it with you. Before leaving the place you have been out at, change your child into a clean nappy (or, if toilet trained, visit the toilet one last time), and have your child put on their pyjamas. Wrap them cosily into their housecoat, and—voilà—no need to wake them up at home to go to bed!

4. Dining? Choose wisely

When choosing a restaurant, plan ahead and choose one that ticks all the boxes for you.

Baby? Make sure there is ample space for a pram or push-chair, as well as a nappy changer.

Toddler? Are there clean highchairs available? If in doubt, take your own compact highchair. Choosing a restaurant with a little bit more space than the norm is ideal, as younger tod-dlers usually do not like being confined to their seats, and you do not want to bother other patrons if you need to walk around with your child a little bit.

School-aged child? Is there a play area to entertain your little one? There are plenty available today. Book early to choose a table close to the area for easy monitoring, or close to a surveillance TV, if available.

5. Kid-proof your table at restaurants

As soon as you sit down, move all cutlery and breakables away from your child's reach. Beware of tablecloths that can be easily pulled by little hands and cause mayhem!

6. Pack some food

Whatever your child's age, it is always a good idea to pack some healthy and familiar snacks and foods. Your child might not be happy with what is available, or might get hungry at an inconvenient time.

7. Pack some containers, too!

You never know how your day is going to turn out with kids! If you're eating out, take an insulated container out with you. It's not the first time my daughter has slept all throughout lunch and has woken out super-hungry the moment we leave! Cut up a portion of food into little pieces and take it away with you.

8. Disposable nappy bags are not just for nappies

These little marvels are lifesavers! They are tiny, and a packet of 20 or so does not take up much space. They can be used for so many things besides dirty nappies!

Here are a few ideas: they can be used to discard dirty wipes and tissues, to hold toys which have fallen on the floor and need a wipe, to hold dummies which have also fallen on the floor, to pack dirty or used cutlery or bottles in, to hold soiled clothes until you get home...and so much more!

9. Keep them entertained

Organise some small 'fun packs' to keep your kids happy and busy when you are out. If you're eating out, you can include playdough, colouring books and colours, sticker packs, small cars or dolls, little puzzles, or small games. If you're out for some fresh air, a bottle of bubbles, a small ball, or a bike or scooter is bound to keep them happy!

10. Pack a 'just in case' bag

The mother of all tips! This bag is to be kept in the car, 'just in case'. Here is what I like to pack in mine: thicker or lighter jackets in case the weather changes, scarves, spare clothes, an extra snack and drink, and a spare dummy, blanket and nappies (when my children were babies).

11. Make the most of it

If you are out and have no set commitments and your toddler falls asleep in the car—hurrah! Do not think about waking your child up. Instead, park somewhere decent and let your little one catch up on their sleep for some time. If you are with your better half, get yourselves a coffee and enjoy each other's company for a while. If you're alone, whip out your e-book reader and enjoy a quiet read!

CELEBRATING THE HOLIDAYS

The holidays can be as stressful as they can be fun, if not more! Being mindful and being prepared for the season ahead will relieve the pressure and will give you ample time and breathing space to focus on what really matters: the actual holiday!

Major holidays such as Christmas

Tips for the working mum

1. Plan a calendar in advance

This will help you to not pack in too much. Space out major commitments and include the most important 'events' and outings before you say yes to the less important things.

2. Order your gifts online

Think ahead and beat the Christmas rush. Who wants to be making hasty last minute shopping trips to buy the last few gifts two days before Christmas? Start making purchases months in advance and get the gifts wrapped immediately, I order everything in October. That way you have more free time on your hands to actually enjoy the season!

3. Start a family tradition

Think simple, such as a family photo with Santa at the mall every year, or attending a Christmas choir evening, or making an event out of gift wrapping. Ours is pancakes in our jammies on Christmas morning and a family photo before we head out the door. Your yearly family tradition will make you feel like you've done 'something' for Christmas!

4. Dealing with family

Being with extended family over the holidays is fun, but stressful too might I add. Decide on a code word with your children for when they need a break from it all. Nothing too obvious, just something to signal they need to leave and have some time off instead of having them get worked up and squabbling with the cousins.

5. Naptimes

Try to stick to your kids' regular naptimes. Large events can be very exhausting for children, and skipping naptimes will only mean that they will become overtired; which is not fun for them or you!

6. Stick with your daily routine

If you're home for Christmas, try to give priority to the things that matter most to you, such as quality time with the kids at home, exercising, or reading, and do not try to squeeze in too much. Trying to do so will leave you feeling overwhelmed and over-worked at the end of it all.

CELEBRATING MINOR HOLIDAYS

Just 10 to 20 minutes the evening before a minor holiday, such as Halloween, or Valentine's Day, is enough time to give your house a little taste of the holiday in question. A few well-intentioned actions create such a sense of fun, especially for the children, and will make an otherwise normal day feel special.

Celebrate minor holidays the easy way. Here are a few ideas:

Halloween, 31st October

- Use orange or black napkins for dinner.

- Use red food colouring to colour the toilet water red.

- Surprise your kids by smiling to show off fake fangs or turning around with a scary mask on!

- Decorate a couple of mason jars with some permanent marker, and light up little candles inside the jars.

Valentine's Day, 14th February

- Draw hearts on the napkins used for breakfast using a permanent marker.

- Use a heart cookie cutter to cut up sandwiches into little hearts.

- Put a little note into their lunchbox telling your kids how much you love them and wishing them a happy Valentine's Day.

- Hang a couple of red balloons inside the house.

GIFTING

Gift giving should be meaningful and fun for both the giver and the receiver. More often than not, gifting takes on a more materialistic sense rather than an intentional and thoughtful way to celebrate someone or something. A few quick tips can help you buy the right gifts with little effort and maximum fun.

1. Keep a list

Use a digital or paper notebook to make lists for different people and holidays. Take note of ideas, and gifts already bought.

2. There's no perfect gift

We often search high and low for the perfect gift, when, in reality, there is no perfect gift. Do not focus on buying a sensational gift for a grand reveal. Instead, focus on buying something useful or meaningful.

3. Enjoy the buying process

Do not shop last minute and rush around buying anything that comes to hand just for the sake of buying a gift. Plan ahead and be intentional.

4. Think about the receiver

Have a little think about who is on the receiving end. What makes them happy? Do they have any favourite movies, bands, colours? A little thinking can go a long way.

5. Buy online

Think of how many virtual stores you can visit in an hour versus how many physical stores you can manage in the same time! Most shops today offer an online option. If your favourite store does not, contact them via social media or by phone to check the stock of what you are after. More often than not, the staff will be more than happy to set your gifts aside to make for an easier pick-up.

6. Buy all year round

This is the ultimate tip. When you're window shopping, or browsing websites, always think about your loved ones. If you come across something which you think someone will love, buy it on the spot, put it away safely in your 'gift stash' area, and take note in your gift notebook.

7. Shop the sales

You can save a ton of money by buying gifts during the sales. If you are not the type to think ahead so much, shop the Black Friday sales online!

8. Keep an SOS gift stash

Use this for all the times we try so hard, but slip up and forget! We're only human after all! This tip will save you time, money, and headaches. Buy some 'generic' gifts such as pretty accessories for women, aftershaves for men, a few art boxes for kids, and a couple of boxes of chocolates. I'm sure you've all forgotten that your aunt is coming to visit over Christmas for one day this year, or have had your kids invited to a last minute birthday party!

ENTERTAINING

The word 'entertaining' sounds so daunting, but do not let it throw you off balance! Entertaining needn't mean 'perfect' centrepieces, 'perfect' houses, 'perfect' dinnerware or 'perfect' three-course meals. Sorry, Martha Stewart!

The scope of entertaining

The scope of entertaining is opening your home to your guests to make them feel comfortable and welcome. Do you really think that having your house look like it was just shot for a home magazine will have your guests feel at ease, especially if they have their children with them? I'm sure you do not enjoy going over to a friend's house if you knew she had to sacrifice a weekend with her kids to plan the perfect dinner party. Just the thought would make you uncomfortable.

Complicating and raising the bar on entertaining will only make you want to do it less, which is a pity, because if done right, entertaining can be easy to do and so much fun!

Easy ways to entertain

- If you're cooking, choose foods that can be cooked in advance. Do not try to cook everything in one day!

- Make one great main dish, and buy some ready-made sides, such as potato salad, and coleslaw.

- Another great hack is to choose foods which do not require much work whilst your guests are at your home, so you are able to join in the fun. Foods served cold, or platters such as cheese or cold cuts are great. One pot dinners, or anything which is popped into the oven and simply cut and served, are also fitting options.

- When your guests ask what they should bring with them, don't be shy. You can nicely say, *"Dessert would be great!"*

- Cook oven food in disposable tin trays and discard after use.

- Organise a potluck or a 'bring-a-dish' party. Pre-assign dishes to everyone, or make it even more fun, and let everyone bring what they want!

- Entertaining needn't mean cooking up fancy food. Think simple plates of pasta, burgers, tacos or anything which may be chucked into the oven for an hour and plated.

- Opt for a pizza and wine night. Buy the pizza and get it delivered and sit back and enjoy the company.

- Make sure the dishwasher is empty right before an event at home.

- If you really can't be bothered to do anything at all, buy some nice disposable plates, servingware, and cutlery, and throw it all away when you're done! This is perfect for larger crowds or a casual summer barbecue.

- Organise a movie night. Think popcorn, sodas, candy, and the family on the sofa—you're done!

- Do not apologise for having a less than perfect house. Your guests will not notice, so don't make it a thing!

CELEBRATING THE KIDS' BIRTHDAYS

A child's birthday is so exciting and special to us mums that we sometimes forget that most of the time, what is most important to your children is definitely not the same as what is most important to us. We often throw parties for us, and not for the kids!

Try to forget about throwing the perfect birthday party; what matters to children the most is the company, the games... and the presents! Even more so, if your child is very little, say one to three or four years, they really don't care much. The exact opposite is true—organising a large party in a foreign environment may trigger clinginess and anxiety.

Here are a couple of age-appropriate party ideas and tips:

First to third birthday party

1. Home is the ideal location. Your child will appreciate not being taken out of their familiar environment.

2. Party size should be small. Very close family and a few close friends of the child should be invited. Avoid inviting people who are not close to the birthday child.

3. Go easy on the decor! Your child will not appreciate or remember the decor you spent hours slaving away on. Include a favourite toy or two on the cake table and have some balloons running around on the floor. If you have to decorate, focus on one area where a pretty birthday photo can be taken. The most convenient place is the cake table.

4. Food should be simple to serve and to eat. Avoid messy foods and complicated recipes that will deter you from spending time with your child. Cold finger foods are the best!

5. Give someone a camera and ask them to take a couple of photos. You will most probably be too busy to do so. Do not forget to do this—you will have some wonderful memories to look back on!

6. For this age group, kids' entertainment might backfire in that young children will not feel comfortable with someone they do not know, trying their best to make them smile. Turn on some nursery rhymes instead, and have the children dance, or have circle time and a singalong.

7. Keep it short. Parties should not last longer than 90 minutes.

8. Timing is key. Schedule the party time for morning or late afternoon after your child has napped. A cranky kid does not make for a good party host!

9. Cut the cake as soon as all the guests arrive so that everybody, especially the birthday kid, still looks presentable. Then serve the cake in due time.

Fourth to seventh birthday party

1. At this age, kids have circles of friends. If you are to throw them a birthday party, invite the friends over the aunt who is not so close to your son or daughter. You can opt to organise a small cake-cutting event at the grandparents on a separate day for close family members, so no one

feels left out.

2. If you decorate, focus on a theme your child loves, such as a favourite cartoon or colour. Elaboration is often not appreciated, but the thought is.

3. Serve simple food kids enjoy and do ask parents to inform you of any allergies when you send out the invitations.

4. Plan for a party that lasts about two hours.

5. An entertainer can be a good idea for this age group. You may also organise some easy and fun games such as musical chairs, musical statues, or pass the parcel, with a few small prizes thrown in.

Age seven onwards

1. Get the kids involved! Parties at this age take on greater meaning.

2. Older kids need more stimulation. Organise sports games, card games, and mystery games.

3. Food can be a little more fun! At this age kids are less picky and can eat without making a mess.

4. An extra hand to help is not a bad idea. Due to a larger group of guests, a sibling or family member can attend to serving drinks whilst you greet guests at the door, for example.

5. Consider serving a number of 'self-service' foods and drinks, so the guests can help themselves.

A party needn't be the only way one celebrates a birthday.

A family outing to mark the occasion, or an intimate birthday breakfast with cake is perfectly fine too!

Some quick tips and ideas for celebrating birthdays

- Decorate the birthday child's bedroom with balloons and streamers whilst they are at school and greet them with a 'Happy Birthday' song as they walk through the door.

- If you're usually not the one picking up or watching your child straight after school or nursery, why not make it extra special by surprising your child and picking them up from school yourself? Take them to their favourite diner, play area, or coffee shop and spend some precious time with them at their favourite spot!

- Make the birthday child a birthday crown or button to wear on their special day.

- Cook their favourite dinner, or ask them what they would like to eat.

- Try to squeeze in an impromptu visit to family or friends so they can be greeted with a *"Happy birthday!"* and be made to feel extra special.

KEY POINTS

1. Do not leave gifts, celebrations, and holiday planning to the last minute. Plan ahead to avoid getting stressed out.

2. A vacation means having a break from it all. You can do this in the simplest of ways.

3. When holidaying, plan, plan, and plan some more. And think again. Making wise decisions will enable you to enjoy it to the full.

4. The actual travelling part can be made so much easier with a little thought. The right games, food, and attitude can ease the hard parts.

5. Entertaining is essentially inviting people you enjoy spending time with into your home to spend quality time with. How you entertain is not a priority. The more comfortable your guests are, the more everyone will enjoy it.

6. Do not go overboard with your child's birthday party. Make sure that whatever you are planning is age-appropriate, and that whatever you are up to is being planned not for your own sake, but for your child's!

Let's have some fun, mum!

EPILOGUE
PARTING THOUGHTS

Now that you have read this book, I do hope that you feel you have learnt some useful and practical strategies which will help you to organise your life both at home and at work.

I like to think that if you had been ignoring yourself before, you are now high on your priority list. *You* matter, more than you ever cared to admit. Always make happiness your strong suit.

Bringing it all together

1. Priorities change. Today it might be getting into shape, to-morrow it might be working on a home revamp. Whatever it is, your time and dedication can be shifted to suit your needs and desires.

2. Take shortcuts where you can. Shortcuts will help you accommodate your priorities.

3. Perfect doesn't exist. Reframe the word 'perfect' to signify whatever works for you and your family.

4. We all get tired. God knows we try (and manage!) to do so much. When you're tired, take it as a sign that you need to slow down. Give yourself some TLC; it might be as simple as a warm cuppa, a book, and an early night.

5. Learn to say 'yes'. If someone offers to pick up the kids, buy you some groceries, or lend a hand, say yes! The person on the other end wouldn't be offering if they weren't willing to pitch in.

6. And learn to say 'no'. We cannot take on more than we can handle, and never ever let anyone put you in a posi-tion where you have to say yes. It might be your kids, your

parents, your partner, your boss...if anyone asks something of you and you are not sure whether you can accommodate them, let that person know you need to have a little think and will get back to them soon. Ask yourself if the request is reasonable and doable before making any commitments.

7. When it comes to parenting, enjoy every moment. Time goes by so fast and, before you know it, your kids are older and out of the house. Cherish the little things, because they will be gone before you know it.

8. Prepare to be judged, but don't let it faze you. People will comment on your crying toddler making a scene, give you looks of disapproval because God forbid your child is happily playing with a tablet whilst you shop in peace, or have the audacity to tell you that you didn't dress him or her warmly enough for the weather. Don't bat an eyelid when they do so.

9. Trust your instincts. There is nothing more powerful than a mother's intuition. Learn to listen to your gut and believe that you can 'detect' things no one else can.

I am positive that you are feeling less overwhelmed and more in control of your life, and have managed to find yourself just a little bit more at each turn of the page.

Dear mamas, your children are incredibly lucky to have you in their lives! Here's to a happier, more fulfilling life!

About the author

Nakita Attard Vassallo is a career girl by day, and a writer and blogger by night, and a mother, wife, and homemaker around the clock.

Born and raised in Malta, Nakita enjoys reading, writing, photography, travel, food, and life in general.

Time management and organising skills are two of Nakita's strong suits. She is intent on helping other mums to benefit from these methods in order to create more time for themselves. Mums need to take care of themselves before taking care of others—and this is something Nakita truly believes in.

Nakita launched the successful blog 'the Mama Manual - A blog for busy mamas' in January 2018.